SpringerBriefs in Finance

SpringerBriefs present concise summaries of cutting-edge research and practical applications across a wide spectrum of fields. Featuring compact volumes of 50 to 125 pages, the series covers a range of content from professional to academic. Typical topics might include: a timely report of state-of-the art analytical techniques, a bridge between new research results, as published in journal articles, and a contextual literature review, a snapshot of a hot or emerging topic, an in-depth case study or clinical example, and a presentation of core concepts that students must understand in order to make independent contributions. SpringerBriefs in Finance showcase emerging theory, empirical research, and practical application in corporate finance, banking, financial management, behavioral finance, financial markets, social and entrepreneurial finance, microfinance, and related fields, from a global author community. Briefs are characterized by fast, global electronic dissemination, standard publishing contracts, standardized manuscript preparation and formatting guidelines, and expedited production schedules.

More information about this series at http://www.springer.com/series/10282

Jörn H Bühring

Private Banking and Wealth Management Futures 2030

Greater China Perspectives

Springer

Jörn H Bühring
Hong Kong Polytechnic University
Hong Kong, China

ISSN 2193-1720 ISSN 2193-1739 (electronic)
SpringerBriefs in Finance
ISBN 978-981-16-3394-2 ISBN 978-981-16-3395-9 (eBook)
https://doi.org/10.1007/978-981-16-3395-9

This Springer imprint is published by the registered company Springer Nature Singapore Pte Ltd.
The registered company address is: 152 Beach Road, #21-01/04 Gateway East, Singapore 189721, Singapore

Preface

University-Industry Collaboration

Ignite Innovation—A Program Initiative of the Hong Kong PolyU School of Design

Ignite Innovation is an initiative of the Hong Kong Polytechnic University's School of Design (SD). The programs' primary goal is to bridge industry needs and academic capabilities, and to showcase the capacity of designers to engage in research, analysis, strategy, visualization, innovation, and concept demonstrations.

Aware of a global shift in consciousness, we recognize the necessity to adapt and create new sustainable value across economic, environmental, social, and public dimensions.

We consider strategic and human-centric design as a starting point in the innovation cycle. Directed and advanced by experts across industry, business and academic communities, design-led innovation is evolving around identified and yet unidentified needs. Working in collaboration with intended users of systems, products, services, and experiences, we endeavour to identify opportunities and co-create sustainable value.

While we are taking unswerving steps toward these goals, continual awareness is created around all affected by Ignite Innovation's positive outcomes.

This "Delphi Study" initiative signifies the continuation of Ignite innovation's collaborative program, which was made possible through the partnership with a global industry leader in financial services, asset management, and investment banking. The main focus of this project was to develop a deeper understanding of the forward-looking perspectives that are relevant to the organization, the industry, market and consumer, and existing and emerging issues that may impact the futures of private banking and wealth management propositions (greater China) to the year 2030.

For more information about this study, or the Ignite Innovation program, please contact:

Dr. Jörn H Bühring
Assistant Professor
Ignite Innovation Program Leader
Delphi Study—Principal Investigator and Author
PolyU School of Design
Hong Kong, China
e-mail: joern.buehring@polyu.edu.hk

Acknowledgements

The PolyU School of Design (SD)—Ignite Innovation program team wishes to acknowledge the contribution of the Delphi expert panel, and the academic advisors, research support staff, and collaborators who were engaged in this invaluable futures study.

Particularly, we are grateful to our research sponsor and the project leadership extended from the partner organization. We sincerely thank everyone for their kind assistance throughout this 10-month project.

Finally, we would also like to express our sincere appreciation for the unnamed supporters who assisted us in some way during the varying project stages of this futures study.

Name of Project: Ignite Innovation Industry Collaboration—(H-ZG4T)
Project Leader: Dr. Jörn Bühring, Delphi Study Principal Investigator and Author
SD Program Leader: Dr. Jörn Bühring, Assistant Professor, Ignite Innovation Program Leader

SD Program—Project Support Committee

Prof. Cees de Bont
Prof. Ilpo Koskinen
Prof. Timothy Jachna
Prof. Lee Tak Chi

SD Project—Research Support Team

Ms. Sravanti Peri, Research Associate
Ms. Tina Lu, Research Assistant

SD Project—Report Illustrations Design Team

Ms. Piyanoot Akkarathammakul, Graphics

Mr. Pan Chen, Illustrations—Prelude
Mr. Nury Vittachi—Storyteller—Prelude

Project Research Advisors

Dr. Joseph Voros, Strategic Foresight, Swinburne University of Technology

Prelude

Private Bank 2030: The Human Factor

A top young media star takes a job in a next-generation private bank and is intrigued to see how banking has evolved.

Eleni Zhao Lai

She IS the zeitgeist, which makes her their best chance of seeing the future

Frank Castor

Node chief Frank is a plugged-in bank boss like no other

Pamela Xi Chen
Pamela has her finger on the pulse of the world's biggest economy

Ah-Lum Lo
Tech-chief Ah-Lum switches seamlessly between humans and AI

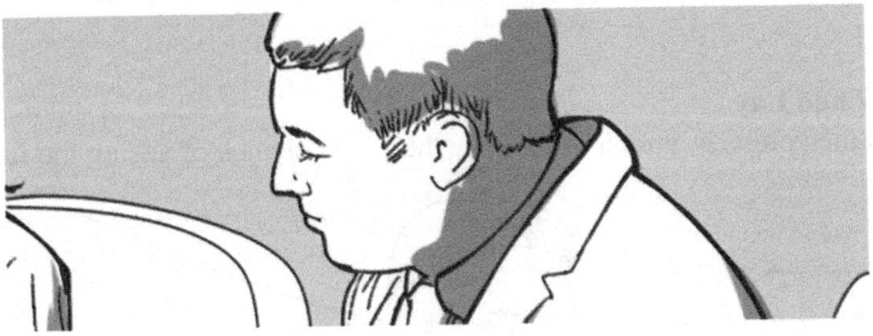

Aditi Das
The data miner knows whom to sign up in partnership deals

Private Bank 2030: The Human Factor

A top young media star takes a job in a next-generation private bank and is intrigued to see how banking has evolved.

THE SUN DOESN'T SHINE in Hong Kong. It attacks.

Eleni Zhao Lal, 16, flies down the sweltering street on her hoverboard, leaning steeply into the breeze to maximize acceleration, lower her body temperature, and—let's be honest here—because it looks cool.

She closes her eyes to fully appreciate the wind on her cheeks, the glow of the sun through her eyelids, and to hear the humming, blood-rushing music of the super-city.

Seconds later, a change in the quality of the sound tells her that she has entered a more open area and a thought in her head, not her own, whispers three words: "You have arrived." She twists her legs like a skier and brings the hoverboard to a halt.

What she sees when she opens her eyes puzzles her.

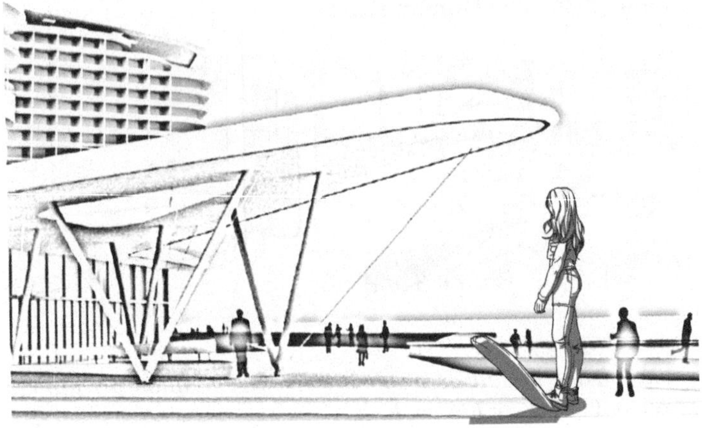

SHE EXPECTED TO BE in the business district. Instead, the floating platform has brought her to a street of open-air cafes near the ocean, a short walk from the gleaming glassy steel towers of the mega-corporations.

"Where am I?" she asks out loud.

Her net-linked earring processes the question and feeds the answer directly into her head by sending audio waves through her skull. "You are outside the IceWave Coffee House. Your meeting is inside in three minutes."

She tucks the board under her arm and steps into the café.

"Good morning, Ms. Zhao Lal," says a greeter, the deadness in his eyes revealing that he is an artificial intelligence-powered hologram. "Your new colleagues are waiting for you at booth 23."

The young woman doesn't respond—she refuses to small-talk with AIs on principle—but marches briskly through the cafe, glancing at everyone she passes, committing everything to memory.

Eleni Zhao Lal is a seer.

IN 2030, PRIVATE BANKS have all but disappeared. The most forward-looking of them all has evolved into a knowledge network manned by tight teams in key nodes around the world.

Analysts describe the teams as "client-facing identities backed by powerful backend platforms", but she prefers to think of the wetware super-processor teams as people.

Eleni knows she will be part of a team known as "boosters", specialists in increasing the net-worth of clients. Booster teams always include chipheads, the experts in big data mining; connectors, the dealmakers who create strategic partnerships; inter-facers, the geeks who create open architecture platforms; and seers, the super-networkers whose job it is to flow with the zeitgeist and know what's coming: that's her.

But as Eleni steps into private room 23, she is aware that there have been rumors that this group's knowledge system is no longer the only successful game in town. Is this famously nimble network in trouble?

ELENI ZHAO LAL, I PRESUME?" says a man of about 30, rising to his feet and putting out a hand.

"You must be Frank Castor," she responds.

The exchange is pure ritual, as each carries discreet AI tools giving them access to real time analysis of the immediate environment.

After introducing her to other members of the team, Castor starts the meeting with a quick outline of how alternative strategies, such as massive computerization of financial technology, were challenging their position as the fastest growing force in finance. Aggressive dinosaur banks were spending a fortune to buy market share, hoping that a leadership position would bring them clients.

"Our rival in China is issuing all their financial advisory teams with miniaturized supercomputers, each of which have 'the power of a human brain', according to the claims they are issuing on the net," he adds. "Each is wired to perform 225 million billion interactions, just like a human brain. From today, humans like us are obsolete, they say. Our rivals are also teaming up with data-rich e-commerce juggernauts, to try to become the biggest players."

Worrying words—but they contrasted with the quiet smile playing on his face.

"Being the biggest doesn't make you the best, right?" Eleni offered.

A red-haired woman who had been introduced as Pamela Xi Chen leaned into the conversation. "Correct. Computers are modular machines which work in serial format," she said. "Brains are massively parallel in structure. The human mind is nothing like a silicon chip. It's more like a quantum field."

Castor added: "Our whole network is run like the synapses in the human brain. We operate, globally, like many minds forming a single super- mind. That's what makes us unbeatable."

AFTERWARDS, ELENI WAS TAKEN to meet the support members of the node, each of whom outlined their special focus.

The tech department was a cluster of casually dressed individuals at the back of the café.

"Smaller teams, bigger flexibility," Castor explained, introducing her to a young man named Ah-Lum.

"We use tech to reduce the need for human interactions across non-critical touch-points," said Lum. "But we've only done so to free up staff to provide more direct interaction with clients. Services are intelligently switched between robo-advisory automation and bespoke human advisory services."

She nodded, and he returned her smile. "Technology is a Faustian bargain," he said. "Every time you gain something, you lose something. But most people never realize that."

In the next booth, she met experts in big data mining and the dealmakers who created strategic partnerships.

The woman in charge, a small south Asian named Aditi, said their findings led them to make many changes, some of which were surprising. "We've moved away from the old client segmentation model to one that is geared to the needs, talents and aspirations of the individual. Other banks fight over ultra-high net worth individuals."

"We don't?" Eleni asked, feeling that it was expected of her.

Aditi smiled. "We don't have to. We create new ultra-high net worth individuals every day."

AFTER SHAKING A FEW more hands, Eleni Zhao Lal was feeling inspired and wanted to get to work. "Is that the end of the tour?"

"There's one more sector you should familiarize yourself with," Castor said. It's the most important of all."

She was puzzled when he led her out of the suite of booths rooms at the back of the coffee shop.

He points to a couple sitting with their child at a table near the main window.

"Meet the Chinese consumer," Castor said. "These individuals are digitally adept and working hard to integrate into global society. They're selective about getting good products and services, but they're also aware of societal issues such as inequality. Yet there's so much to think about, and so much information overload, that they no longer just trust the media or go for brand names. They need the advisor who can see their needs and the big picture at the same time. They need influencers, thought-leaders, trend-setters. They need you."

Eleni noticed that the family were chuckling at something they were watching on a tablet. "I hope that's one of my videos," she said.

"Very likely. You're number one in China, right? Questions, comments?"

She bit her bottom lip. "Well, you know, my father was in banking technology. In those days people thought computerization would solve everything," she mused.

"Technology makes a great employee but a terrible boss," Castor said. "The key element is the human spirit. Sometimes it's best not to think too much. You just have to feel your way forwards."

Eleni thought of her journey that morning, flying down the street on her hoverboard, eyes tightly shut, making herself hyper-aware of light and sound and sensation.

"I think I'm going to like it here," she said.

THE END

Contents

Chapter 1
Introduction

Abstract In this chapter, the main arguments are put forward as to why leaders in design and business innovation must not only adapt to the current circumstances, but to think of, and prepare for the future. With the emphasis placed on multi-disciplinary teams having to work together to identify with macro and micro trends from which user engagement opportunities and possibilities for consumer-directed value creation, the emergence of new approaches toward imagining preferable futures are highlighted. The chapter puts forward the notion that developing a deeper understanding of the forward-looking perspectives which are relevant to Private Banking and Wealth Management futures (greater China) to the year 2030. Here, the Delphi method is introduced, which was used as a process to engage with a cohort of business and academic experts with specific knowledge in the field to arrive at a set of preferable wealth management futures scenarios. Statements of the study objectives are presented, and the chapter concludes with an outline of the research report outline and its contents.

Keywords Uncertainty · Visioning · Learning-based collaboration · Delphi method · Action-oriented foresight

We are living in times of rapid change and transformation where organizations and individuals are being challenged not only to adapt to current circumstances, but to think of, and prepare for the future. Taking steps toward gaining a deeper understanding of current and future opportunities and possibilities, requires—foremost, vision and leadership that enables organizational collaboration both internally and externally. To this end, The Polytechnic University—School of Design in partnership with a global industry leader, have set out to develop a shared understanding that Design (principles, methods, and processes) can indeed play a significant role in organizational leadership, innovation, and new value creation. This applied research and design led innovation program operates under the identity of "Ignite Innovation".

In August 2015, the first project of this unique University-Industry partnership program took place: "Project 1" involved a selected group of Master and Bachelor degree students from various Design disciplines. Supported and coached by academia, multi-disciplinary design professionals engaged full-time over a period of four consecutive months with stakeholders from the partner organization and their

J. H. Bühring, *Private Banking and Wealth Management Futures 2030*,
SpringerBriefs in Finance, https://doi.org/10.1007/978-981-16-3395-9_1

selected client representations. The outcome depicts a new generation (Millennials) of future Wealth Management and private banking users, and their related product-, service-, and experiential needs, wants, and forward-looking aspirations.

Inspirations derived from these initial learnings, and gaining valuable insights into, for example, industry (business) practices, macro and micro trends from which user engagement opportunities and possibilities for consumer-directed value creation emerged, the program has evolved to this next phase of engagement. **Welcome to "Project 2—Private Banking and Wealth Management Futures 2030—A Design Foresight Delphi study—Greater China Perspectives"**, where the underlining objectives were to develop ambitious forward-looking perspectives from which we lay the groundwork for accelerated collaborative learning, visioning, strategizing, and design led innovation.

1.1 Inventing Preferable Futures—Why is this Important?

It is widely believed that we are in a critical juncture in human history, and speculations abound as to what is likely to lead to contrasting futures. World Leaders, Governments, Industries, and human agencies are foreshadowing mega trends, industrial revolutions, giant leaps in science and technology, game-changers, and fundamental forces (both macro and micro) that only add to the organizational complexity of dealing with uncertainties. To illustrate the urgency, we may assume that all industries are a bell curve, and that all industries have a beginning, a middle, and eventually head towards an end; that is, before they (in some new form) re-enter a new bell curve, or simply seize to exist. It is believed that most industries are currently at the declining end of the curve (Fig. 1.1) and are being challenged by some form of disruption.

With this visualization in mind, the future is not a linear extension of what we are doing today, instead, new connections will need to be made between events and trends that might still be invisible on the organization's radar. Fundamentally, however, futures are impossible to predict and are not set in stone, hence, it will

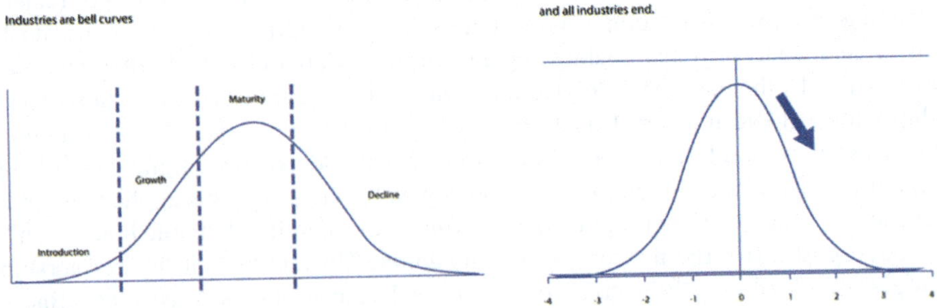

Fig. 1.1 Normal probability distribution of an industry maturity cycle

require leadership and empowerment to instill an exploratory mindset and a *no regret* philosophy when envisaging alternative futures.

The best we can do is imagine the future by thinking about change in five dimensions:

- Examining and projecting current trends and issues.
- Considering potential events or tipping (inflection) points.
- Developing positive futures.
- Choosing among the options.
- Engaging with multi-disciplinary teams to design, invent, and pilot (prototype) preferred futures.

1.2 Aims and Objectives of Project 2—A Delphi Study

The main focus of this study project was to develop a deeper understanding of the forward-looking perspectives that are relevant, and those that may impact the future of Private Banking (greater China) to the year 2030, and its broader wealth management proposition. That is, by soliciting the views of industry experts as to what are the current issues that determine growth or potential decline (collapse) and trying to sense possible events through early signals that might impact the organization, the industry and its markets. Furthermore, proffering the increasing relevance of design led innovation, another key objective of this study was to elicit experts' opinions on the evolving consumer perspective in context of the study topic.

Indeed, the technological and cultural changes that we experience as highly disruptive today, form the foundational assumptions of the next consumer generation's worldviews. Their identities are extended through social media and civil upheaval, and their problem-solving skills are forged in online forums with millions of global participants. Moreover, the next consumer generations economic priorities are framed by a fragmented global economy, mass automation of existing industries, and the existential threats of, for example, climate change and an unsustainable economy. In this transformational environment, how will this generation of consumers make their investment decisions, and specifically, how will privacy and security be valued by a generation such as Millennials? Moreover, how will this affect the 18-year-olds today that in a decade from now, will be taking on positions of leadership in our largest institutions? In other words, what does their experience of the world today tell us about how they may reshape our society tomorrow.

Consequently, expert opinions to these and other questions may help us envisage and inform the invention of a preferred private banking eco-system to the year 2030. To deal with this topic, this Ignite Innovation industry collaboration project (Project 2) thus endeavored to engage with a predetermined group of industry experts in financial services industry and private banking sector, while a smaller group of scholars representing academic discourse were deemed as important, adding to the richness of the findings.

1.3 The Experts as Participants on the Delphi Panel

Involving study participants with high levels of expertise, a group comprising of between 9 and 12 experts was deemed adequate for this study. Representing the views of the Financial Industry, and with a specific knowledge in private banking and wealth management, key stakeholders responsible for strategy, innovation, product development, marketing, IT, and client engagement, were identified from within the partner organization. Their far-reaching areas of responsibility across local and regional markets in greater China, including representatives with Corporate Leadership positions, gave this study the depth and multi-perspectives outlined in the introduction.

Beyond the organization, however, this project was designed to include a small group of scholars, and the expertise they would bring to the Delphi Panel in terms of social science, technology, and innovation. This approach was deemed as important, as this would potentially provide a more holistic view of the issues and forward-looking possibilities entailed in the final outcomes of this project.

In total, 12 experts (10 from industry, and 2 from academia) took part in the initial scoping round of the survey (Table 1.1).

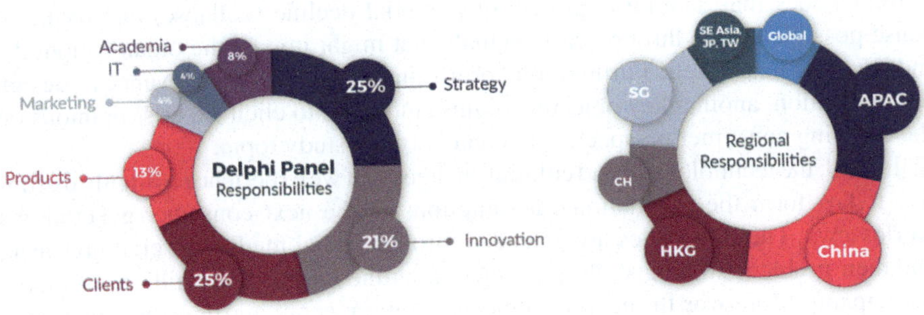

Table 1.1 Delphi expert panel, functional and regional responsibilities

Delphi study	
Number of expert participants	12
Data collection method	Delphi (via online survey)
Survey rounds	2
Age range	30–60
Years of experience in financial industries	1–15+
Average years of experiences (panel)	11.5

1.4 The Data Collection Method (Delphi)

The Delphi technique is an interactive forecasting method for obtaining consensus, which has been successfully used in science, technology and business-related fields. During the Delphi process, experts were asked to answer questions in two or more rounds (Fig. 1.2); after each round, the Delphi moderator responded with an anonymous summary of all participant's answers and arguments provided for their judgment. As a qualitative research method, the aim is to take advantage of one its key strength, which is the ability to gather opinions from experts from different backgrounds, and use it to identify contextual trends, ideally, leading to preferred futures in private banking. Amongst its many advantages, the Delphi method allows experts to remain anonymous and to be geographically dispersed during the project phase. Hence, mindful of participants' busy schedules, this project adopted a web-based Delphi survey tool, which means that participants were able to interact remotely around the subject topic without having to physically meet as a group.

A key output of this project was **logical and useful statements (scenarios) about desired futures,** which allows forecasting, comparing, and indeed creating of new and innovative concepts to transpire. Beyond the outcomes of this project itself, however, lies the believe that ***thinking about the future***—both at external collective levels and inner individual levels—is the first important step toward formulating a process of design-inspired foresight that will lead to the creation (and invention) of preferred futures. Specifically, this project was envisioned:

- **To spark a mindset of action-oriented foresight** that can be manifested in future business practices and processes (conversely, to assess current readiness).
- **To engage key internal stakeholders** responsible for the future prosperity and sustainability of their organization[s].
- **Developing skills that are critical in the longer-term planning** and strategies needed to deal with uncertainty.

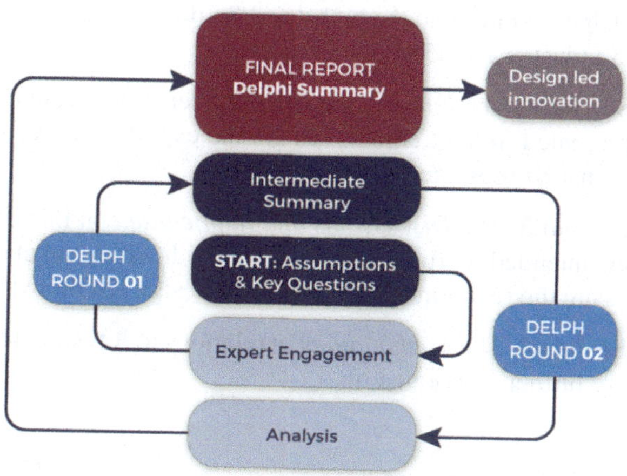

Fig. 1.2 Delphi Survey: Two consecutive rounds with industry and academic experts

- **To encourage an action-oriented approach to creating the future** rather than simply predicting it.
- **To contribute in the strategy formulation process** by establishing divisional and regional milestones and measures.
- **To develop a common mental map of the future** with respect to a Private Bank scenario to the year 2030.
- **To foster creative thinking skills** that allow for multiple interpretations of reality, and where each future scenario is fundamentally different to the other.
- **To develop skills and abilities that allow emerging issues (and disrupters) to be identified** before they become unwieldy and expensive—and, to search for new opportunities and possibilities.
- **To position design as a strategic process** of human-centric innovation applied across eco-systems, communities, organizations, products, services, and user experiences.

At the conclusion of this study, this report summary captures the experts combined insights and opinions, and the consensus reached toward desired futures of private banking propositions. To this end, the report is structured into five sections; a brief outline of each section follows:

Prelude: *Private Bank 2030: The Human Factor*—a narrative of a top young media star who is intrigued to learn how banking has evolved, as she takes up a new position in the next-generation private bank 2030.

Section 1: The *Introduction* provides a brief overview of the aims and objectives of this research project, the research method (Delphi), and the experts that took part in this futures study.

Section 2: *Mega Trends* are introduced that highlight some of the key macro developments affecting important decisions along the path toward the next-generation of the Private Bank.

Section 3: The *Delphi Summary* outlines the research questions for each of the two Delphi rounds, and the high-level findings that emerged from engaging with a group of industry and academic experts.

Section 4: The *Futures Scenarios* that emerged from the two-round Delphi study are presented in their entirety, as are the experts consensus ratings given to each of the scenarios presented.

Section 5: The *Discussions and Implications* of this design-inspired foresight study are intended for further engagement with senior stakeholders within the organization, as are the recommendations toward design led innovation initiatives.

Section 6: The *Methodology* in relations to foresight techniques applied in this study are further elaborated on.

Chapter 2
Mega Trends—Introduction

Abstract What are the mega trends and drivers of change which are likely to have significant impact on business and society to the year 2030? Key trends are presented at a high-level, and discussed for their potential implications.

Keywords Mega trends · Change drivers · STEP factors · Business implications

J. H. Bühring, *Private Banking and Wealth Management Futures 2030*,
SpringerBriefs in Finance, https://doi.org/10.1007/978-981-16-3395-9_2

2.1 What are the Mega Trends which have Major Impact on Business and Society in 2030?

Cities, Population, Energy, Technologies, Digital Transformation, Climate Change

The world is in anticipation of a fourth industrial revolution. This revolution is driven by giant leaps in digital technologies and promises to radically alter the face of industry in the coming decades. The uptake of industrial internet and internet of things (IoT) in manufacturing creates new value chains for traditional industries. Innovations will underline the importance of digital and sustainable business solutions as key drivers for success. How can regional economies and innovation systems respond to this? If entire development and production processes become digital, will regions and cities remain the key spatial units where knowledge is transferred, and competition to attract investments and talents takes place?

And what about the human factor? Scientists have declared that the first person who will live to be 150 years old has already been born. This will bring with it some interesting consequences with, not the least of which is, "How long does he want to work? If he wants to work to 65 and lives to be 150, that's going to be an interesting math equation (DeBord 2016a)".

Millennials, who are already emerging as leaders in technology and other industries, will comprise of 75% of the global workforce by 2025. They want to work for organizations that foster innovative thinking, develop their skills, and make a positive contribution to society (Dobson 2014).

Time is also important. Rich or poor, old or young, we all only have 24 h in a day, and what we do in that time is becoming increasingly precious to us. Digital devices were sold on the premise that they would save us time, but—as some make us believe—that this was the greatest modern scam ever, because they really blur the boundaries between work and home life (DeBord 2016b). The problem, then, is less how much time people have than how they will make best use of the solutions that are on offer to them; think Alexi, Siri et al. as evolving types of personal digital assistants.

2.2 Mega Trends—Global (Athena 2016)

Key Drivers of Change

- Cities
- Population
- Energy
- Technologies
- Digital transformation
- Climate change

Most Affected Sectors
Food, Transport, Construction, Manufacturing, Clothing, Emergency services, **Technology**, **Finance**, Government, Healthcare.

2.3 What is Changing?

Cities

- *By 2030*, the world is projected to have 41 mega-cities with more than 10 million inhabitants each.
- By 2025, out of the top 600 cities in the world in economic terms, more than one hundred will be in China.
- China will contain eight cities of at least 10 million people in the coming decade.
- China is expected to add close to 300 million more urbanites by 2030.

Demographics

- By 2050, the world's urban population will have increased by some 72%.
- By 2050 the population of Asia is expected to be 5.2 billion people accounting for roughly half the world's 10–11 billion population at the time.
- While much attention is focused on China's emerging middle class, consumers in upper middle class and affluent households will have the most impact over the next four years.

Business

- 40% of existing jobs worldwide will be lost by 2020 but many new ones will be created in the high-growth industries.
- Facebook's aggressive move into publishing will disrupt many marketing plans and jeopardize the traditional inbound marketing model.

- By 2030 a small number of companies will begin calculating their labour costs with something called "synoptical currency" (Frey 2016).

Technology

- More change will result from advances in technology in the next five years than has occurred over the past 50 years.
- By the end of 2017, 60% of the top 1000 enterprises in the Asia Pacific will have digital transformation as their core business strategy.
- By 2022, one in every 10 people will be wearing clothes connected to the internet.
- Cash-rich enterprise software companies like Oracle and Microsoft will start to buy up many of the cash-poor data companies.
- Technology will enable virtual versus physical business and operating models.
- Internet of Things [IoT] will grow to become a $1.7 trillion market by 2020.
- Machine learning technologies will make it possible to discover unknown signals.
- Platforms such as big data, analytics and mobility are expected to become the pillars of smart building evolution in terms of technology, business value and customer satisfaction.
- Information stored in the cloud will shoot up to 40% by 2020.
- Industry 4.0-3/4D and additive printing, robots, a circular and sharing economy, and the IoT will change manufacturing forever.

Transportation

- Shared transportation, driverless cars and disruptive technology-related solutions will generate new competition.
- The rise of high-speed rail and people's increasing expectations of airport facilities mean the world will need fewer mega-hub airports.
- Many more mega-growth players will emerge in sectors such as driverless cars.
- Drones will increasingly do many delivery, security and measurement jobs.

Climate Change

- Human-induced climate change will increase storm intensity by between 2 and 11% by the end of the century.

- An increase of global temperatures of 4–6 °C by the end of the century could increase the annual area burned by a factor of two to five

Implications

- The megatrends of digital transformation, globalization, urbanization, demographic change and climate change will provide growth opportunities.
- Three concepts of urbanization will emerge megacities, mega regions and mega corridors.
- Greater information flows will enable more people to become aware of opportunities for work both nearby and in distant places.
- Some of today's large global managers will become mega-managers.

Mega Trends—Asia

According to studies with focus on the East (Policy Horizons Canada 2016), by 2030, about six in ten people on the planet will be living in Asia. With a growing economy and middle-class, Asia is expected to be a key player on the world stage. While the twenty-first century may turn out to be the Asian century, Asia's future trajectory is still uncertain. It is subject to regional social and economic complexities, as well as environmental, technological and political forces in the region and globally. The interactions of these forces can lead to uncertainties and surprises that will shape the region and the world. Given Asia existing and potential influence, an enhanced understanding of Asia and its potential paths forward over the next 10–15 years is needed.

Over the next 15 years, significant changes are taking shape in Asia:

- Asian economic models are evolving, as countries experiment with their own paths to prosperity. There is an early sense that a shift is underway from a GDP-centered model to more inclusive growth models.
- Social inequality, demographic shift is, and growing expectations of a rising middle-class, are challenging governments to respond and prove their legitimacy.
- Emerging technologies might be a potentially a disruptive force in the region. Over time, some Asian leadership in fields such as bio-manufacturing, artificial intelligence, and robotics may emerge or solidify.
- In order to address some of the challenging environmental and energy issues, some governments have demonstrated a willingness to take significant policy measures and support a range of technologies.
- On the security front, Asia is facing potential disruptions from both historically rooted disputes and emerging technologies.

2.4 STEP Factors

Social Trends

- By 2030 over 2 billion jobs will have disappeared, freeing up talent for many new fledgling industries (Frey 2016).
- By 2030 democracy will be viewed as inferior form of government (Frey 2016).
- By 2030 traditional police forces will be largely automated out of existence with less than 50% of current staffing levels on active duty (Frey 2016).
- By 2030 we will have seen a number of global elections with the intent of creating a new global mandate, forcing world leaders to take notice (Frey 2016).
- By 2030 basic computer programming will be considered a core skill required in over 20% of all jobs. (Frey 2016)

- The Individual Empowerment: Highly influential mega trend as it is both the origin and result of other trends. Individual empowerment will considerably increase its speed (National Intelligence Council 2012).

2.5 Population Trends

Higher Life Expectancy and Decline in Birth Rates (KPMG 2014)

- World: Population will reach to 8.3 billion. Growth will be 20% but slowing down compared to the last 20 years.
- Developed: Population will grow by 3.6% from 1.2 billion to 1.3 billion people.
- Developing: Population will grow by 24%, so seven times faster than in the developed countries, from 5.7 billion people to 7.0 billion (National Intelligence Council 2012; Roland Berger Strategy Consultants 2011).
- Growing Global Middle Class (KPMG 2014).
- World: 60% of the world's population will be middle class.
- Developed: 80% of the global middle class will reside in developing countries.

Widespread Aging (National Intelligence Council 2012)

- Age structures will range from extraordinarily youthful populations (25 or younger) to populations that are longer lived than previously thought possible.
- World: Aging will accelerate due to rising life expectancy. Median age will increase by 5.1–34 years.
- Developed: Median age will increase by 4.4–44 years.
- Developing: Median age will increase by 5.5–32 years (Roland Berger Strategy Consultants 2011).

Urbanization (National Intelligence Council 2012)
Faster growth in global migration due to shortage of skilled and unskilled workforce in both developed and developing countries. Slow shift of the highest urbanization growth rate from Asia to Africa.

- World: Urbanization will continue. 59% of the world's population will live in cities.
- Developed: Share of urban population will increase by 5.7 percentage points to 81%.
- Developing: Share of urban population will increase by 9.9 percentage points to 55%. (Roland Berger Strategy Consultants 2011)

Sustainable Development (GCB 2014)
Higher importance to sustainable principles will lead to an established sustainable society (Social Sustainability, Economic Sustainability, and Ecological Sustainability) worldwide including even those countries that never played a lead in sustainable development initially. It will be dominant and continue to be the same.

Growing Food, Water, and Energy Nexus (National Intelligence Council 2012)

- Increasing nexus among food, water and energy will have far-reaching effect on global development.
- Demand for food is set to rise by more 30%.
- Annual global water requirements will reach 6900 billion cubic meters, 40% above current sustainable water supplies.
- Demand for energy will rise dramatically about 50%.

Climate Change Challenges (National Intelligence Council 2012)
More extreme weather will lead to general warming affecting weather and ecosystems, causing increasing impact on humans.

Increase in CO_2 emissions (Roland Berger Strategy Consultants 2011)

- World: CO_2 emissions will increase by 16% while per capita emissions will stay relatively stable at 4.2 t
- Developed: CO_2 emissions will decline by 14%, accounting for 32% of the world's emissions
- Developing: CO_2 emissions will increase by 38% to a global share of 68%.
- Per capita emissions will still be far below those of developed countries (41%).

Global Warming (Roland Berger Strategy Consultants 2011)

- World: The average global temperature will rise, 0.5–1.5 °C
- Developed: Developed countries have more resources to handle the negative consequences of rising temperatures
- Developing: Developing countries will suffer more from the negative consequences of higher temperatures.

Ecosystem at Risk (Roland Berger Strategy Consultants 2011)

- World: Increasing land loss, more extreme weather and decreasing biodiversity
- Developed: Are less affected by loss of species than developing countries, as they already experienced considerable losses in the twentieth century
- Developing: Increasing loss of species by 2030. Agricultural land available per person will decline by 20% to 0.4 acres.

Scarcity of Natural Resources (KPMG 2014)

- The combination pressure of population growth, economic growth and climate change will place increased stress on essential natural resources.
- 50% increase in food production will likely be necessary to feed 8.3 billion populations
- 40% estimated global gap between water supply and demand.
- About 1 billion more people will live in areas of water stress.

Technological Trends

- By 2030 over 10% of all global financial transactions will be conducted through Bitcoin or Bitcoin-like crypto currencies (Frey 2016).
- By 2030 we will see a growing number of highways designated as driverless-vehicle only (Frey 2016).
- By 2030, the world's largest Internet company will be in the education business, and it will be a company we have not heard of yet (Frey 2016).
- By 2030 it will be common to use next generation search engines to search the physical world (Frey 2016).

Technology Diffusion (Roland Berger Strategy Consultants 2011)

- World: Technology diffusion will increase as new technologies are being adopted faster and innovation cycles shorten.
- Developed: Already being on high level technology diffusion will accelerate.
- Developing: Technology diffusion reduces poverty and facilitates doing business even in less developed regions.

Power of Innovation (Roland Berger Strategy Consultants 2011)

- World: Robotics, virtual reality and the Internet of things will change our lives.
- Developed: The Japanese aim to have a robot in every home by 2015; South Korea has the same goal for 2020.
- Developing: will soon catch up in innovation capacity. China's R&D investments will be about 80% higher than Germany's in 2020.

Technological Convergence/The Age of Life Sciences (GCB 2014)

- World: Basic innovations will be expected from Life Sciences, answering some of the world's challenges.
- Developed: Biotechnology is likely to account for nearly 3% of the GDP of OECD countries.
- Developing: These countries will be the main markets for green and white biotechnology, paving the way to sustainable agriculture (Roland Berger Strategy Consultants 2011).
- "Miniaturization and virtualization will drive the convergence between nano, bio, and ICT and cognitive Sciences, spurring innovation and accelerating research and development in many fields".

Economic Trends

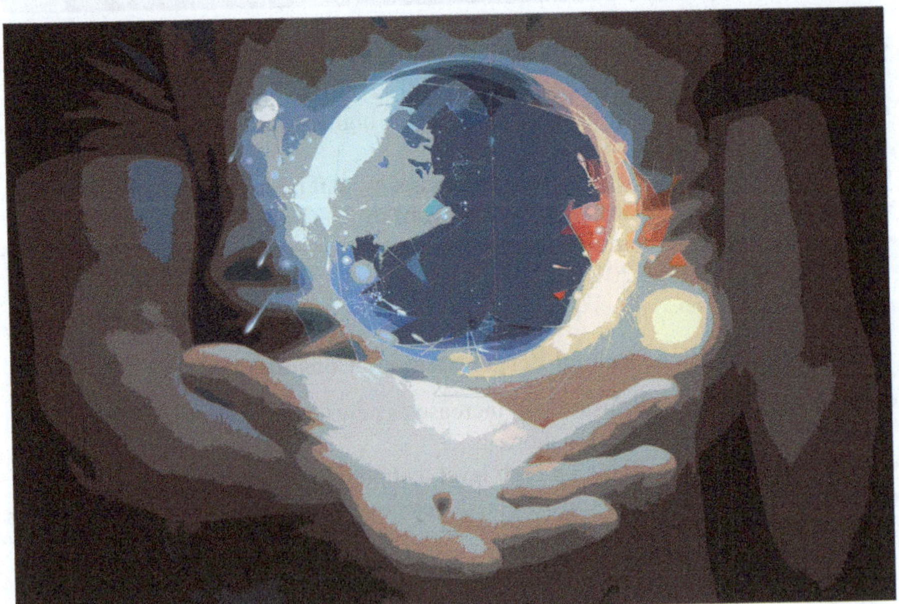

Ongoing Globalization (Roland Berger Strategy Consultants 2011)

- World: Globalization will continue, with real exports growing faster than real GDP (5.3% p.a. vs. 4.0% p.a.).
- Developed: Real GDP is expected to rise by 1.8% per annum—These countries will account for only 27% of global nominal exports.
- Developing: Real GDP will rise by 6.7% per annum—These countries will account for 73% of global nominal exports.

Overwhelming Economic Growth of BRIC Countries (Brazil, Russia, India and China) (Roland Berger Strategy Consultants 2011)

- Economic Growth: Real GDP in the BRIC countries will grow by 7.9% p.a. and exports by 7.8% p.a.
- Market Capitalization: BRIC's equity market cap could rise by 10.6% p.a. to USD 59 trillion.

Economic Power Shift (KPMG 2014)

- Emerging economies are lifting millions out of poverty while also exerting more influence in the global economy.
- Developing countries will be home to 440 of the world's fastest growing cities generating 47% of the global GDP growth.
- China and India will account for 35% of world's population and 25% of global GDP.

Public Debt (KPMG 2014)

- Public debt is expected to operate as a significant constraint on fiscal and policy options.
- Global levels of net public debt are set to reach 98% of GDP.
- An average of 133% of GDP in the Eurozone, 213% of GDP in the US, and 386% of GDP in Japan.
- Population aging will drive up health and pension spending by.
- 4.4% of GDP in developed countries.
- 3.2% of GDP in developing countries.

Political Trends

Diffusion of Power (National Intelligence Council 2012)
There will not be any hegemonic power; Power will shift to networks and coalitions in a multipolar world. Asia will have surpassed North America and Europe combined in terms of global power. China alone will probably have the largest economy surpassing United States. The economies of other non-western countries such as Colombia, Egypt, Indonesia, Iran, South Africa, Mexico, Turkey and others that are middle tier at present could rise by 2030. In terms of economic power, the gap between India and China will begin to close.

The Rise and Fall of Countries (National Intelligence Council 2012
Not the same Old Story: The rapid change of various countries fortunes as much as change themselves will put stresses both on countries conduct with one another and internally as expectations about the position of one's country in the overall international setup are realized or dashed.

Their global power will either level off or the rate of increase of their global power will slow. Not only China and the United States, but also Europe, Japan, and Russia may be passing through inflection points that will translate stress on the international system.

The Limit of Hard Power in the World of 2030 (National Intelligence Council 2012)
By 2030, no country whether the US, China, or any other large country will be a hegemonic power. Enabled by communications technologies, power almost certainly will shift more towards multifaceted and amorphous networks composed of state and non-state actors that will influence global policies of various issues.

The Governance Gap (National Intelligence Council 2012)
The rapid advances in information, communication, and other technologies argue for publics and institutions that will be better able to tackle global and regional challenges. However, the increasing number of powers needed to solve a major transnational challenge will complicate decision-making.

Diffused power will lead to a situation where diverse state, non-state actors and subnational actors (cities) will play an influential governance role.

Potential for Increased Conflict: Interstate conflicts, changing calculations of key players (China, India, and Russia), inclusion of nuclear deterrent as result of future wars in South Asia and Middle East. Islamic terrorism might stop, but terrorism will not vanish completely. Instead with worldwide accessibility to lethal and disruptive technologies, individual specialized in cyber system might sell their services terrorists leading to formation of widespread economies and financial disruptions.

Shift to Global Cooperation (Roland Berger Strategy Consultants 2011)

- World: Global trend among nations to cooperate and share responsibility will intensify.
- Developed: Existing partnerships and institutions will have to react and increasingly adapt to the views of developing countries.
- Developing: The number of economic, trade and social collaborations will increase faster than in developed countries.

Growing Power of NGOs (Roland Berger Strategy Consultants 2011)

- World: The number of NGOs will show double-digit growth rates.
- Developed: The US will remain the forerunner in NGO growth.
- Developing: Experts see clear signs of dynamic growth for community foundations in Africa, Asia and Latin America.

Growth in Humanitarianism (Roland Berger Strategy Consultants 2011)

- World: Philanthropy will grow further on a global level, but the philosophy of giving will change.
- Developed: Private donations will show continuous growth rates.
- Developing: The philanthropic sectors in developing countries will differ. In the more open societies (Brazil, India), a new philanthropic culture will be free to flourish.

References

DeBord M (2016a) Ford has an executive whose entire job is to predict the future. Available at: http://www.businessinsider.com/ford-in-house-futurist-2016-3. Accessed 28 Nov 2016

Dobson S (2014) Big demands and high expectations: 3hat generation Y wants from business, government, and the future workplace. Deloitte UK. Available at: https://www2.deloitte.com/uk/en/pages/press-releases/articles/big-demands-and-high-expectations-what-generation-y-wants.html. Accessed 28 Nov 2016

DeBord, M. (2016b) This Ford exec spends all her time thinking about the future. Available at: http://www.businessinsider.com/ford-in-house-futurist-now-2016-3. Accessed 28 Nov 2016

Policy Horizons Canada (2016) The future of Asia. Available at: http://www.horizons.gc.ca/sites/default/files/Publication-alt-format/ms4-final-en_150dpi_0.pdf. Accessed 28 Nov 2016

Athena (2016) Megatrends. Available at: https://www.shapingtomorrow.com/home/alert/1764754-Megatrends. Accessed 28 Nov 2016

Frey T (2016) 33 Dramatic Predictions for 2030. Available at: http://www.futuristspeaker.com/business-trends/33-dramatic-predictions-for-2030/. Accessed 28 Nov 2016

National Intelligence Council (2012) Global trends 2030 November 2012. Available at: https://globaltrends2030.files.wordpress.com/2012/11/global-trends-2030-november2012.pdf. Accessed 1 Sept 2016

KPMG (2014) Future state 2030. Available at: https://www.kpmg.com/Global/en/IssuesAndInsights/ArticlesPublications/future-state-government/Documents/future-state-2030-v3.pdf. Accessed 1 Sept 2016

Roland Berger Strategy Consultants (2011) Trend Compendium 2030. Available at: https://www.rolandberger.com/gallery/trend-compendium/tc2030/content/assets/trendcompendium2030.pdf. Accessed 1 Sept 2016

GCB (2014) https://www.izt.de/fileadmin/downloads/pdf/GCB_zukunftsstudie_en_final_np.pdf. Available at: https://www.izt.de/fileadmin/downloads/pdf/GCB_zukunftsstudie_en_final_np.pdf. Accessed 1 Sept 2016

Chapter 3
A Delphi Summary of Desired Futures 2020 and 2030

"There is no favorable wind for the man who knows not where he is going." (Seneca, 4 BC – A.D. 65).

Abstract The Delphi method helped develop a deeper understanding of how experts in the fields of private banking, wealth management, technological innovations, and social discourse consider future trends, developments, and related forces likely to lead to opportunities and emerging possibilities in the private banking sector. Qualitative research methods, and the use of foresight processes and tools, are introduced in what the author referrers to as a design-inspired foresight approach. Specifically, this chapter lays out the participant sampling, research design, study questions, and approaches taken to illicit current and emerging issues from experts in Financial Services over several Delphi rounds probing into the future (2020, 2030) from four perspectives:—the organization, market, industry, and the Chinese consumer. The analysis of the Delphi survey produced a total of 237 issues, and 8 scenario statements across two time horizons.

Keywords Research design · Delphi rounds · Design-inspired foresight · Future cone · Backcasting · Consensus · Building · Preferred futures · Futures scenarios

3.1 Study Motivation

There is a growing awareness that business organizations, regardless of industry or size, are faced with unprecedented uncertainties over social analyses, globalization, and technology revolutions, as observed by the increasing interest in future studies. Indeed, some speak of forces so powerful that they will 'transform global systems, social institutions, and our personal lives' (Voros 2003). Simultaneously, a fundamental shift has emerged where access and the value attributed to information is cause of an emerging social structure that presents fundamental challenges for organizations and their understanding of markets and new users within them.

J. H. Bühring, *Private Banking and Wealth Management Futures 2030*,
SpringerBriefs in Finance, https://doi.org/10.1007/978-981-16-3395-9_3

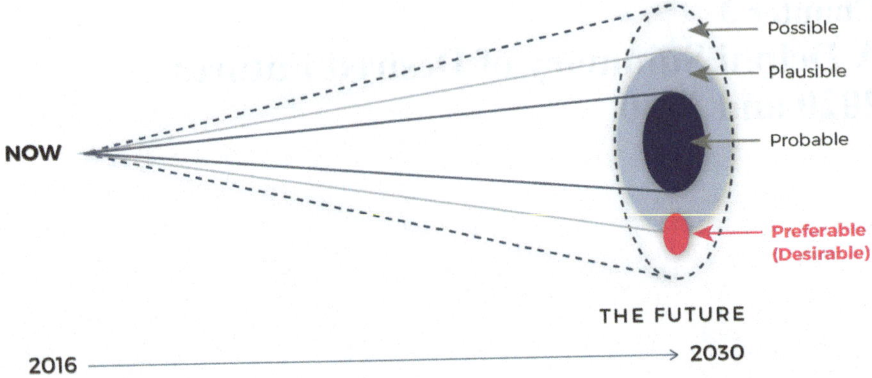

Definitions of Likelihood of Occurrence:

Desirable futures that we "**want to happen**"; these are based on emotional and personal judgements, and are more subjective in nature.

Probable futures that are "**likely to happen**"; often based on the linear continuance of current (present) trends that are still subjective to sudden demise, or unexpectedly emerging new once.

Plausible futures that "**could happen**"; based on our current knowledge of how things (e.g. processes, system of human interactions, physical law, etc.) work.

Possible futures that "**might happen**"; they include all kinds that we can imagine, no matter how far-fetched, and may involve knowledge which we do not yet possess.

Fig. 3.1 Futures cone—graphical representation of four types of alternative futures. [Adapted from Voros (2003), Hancock and Bezold (1994) [14], with definitions for likelihood]

Against this changing business environment, organizations are required to transform themselves, rethink their business models, innovate, and envisage possible, probable, and preferable futures (Fig. 3.1) in order to adapt their approach to business, and indeed the way they engage with now vastly empowered consumers.

To be successful, however, organizations must learn new management practices that enable them to look beyond the horizon and interpret trends, drivers of change, wild cards, discontinuity, amid a constant lookout for weak signals that are often the first important indicators of looming issues and probable change. As ancient wisdom suggests, *'there is no favorable wind for the man who knows not where he is going'* (Seneca, 4 BC – A.D. 65).

The aim of this project was to develop a deeper understanding of how experts in the fields of private banking, wealth management, technological innovations, and social discourse consider future trends, developments, and related forces likely to lead to opportunities and emerging possibilities in the private banking sector. To accomplish this ambitious task of looking beyond the horizon to the year 2030, we relied on the tacit knowledge of executives with privileged access to relevant information, or

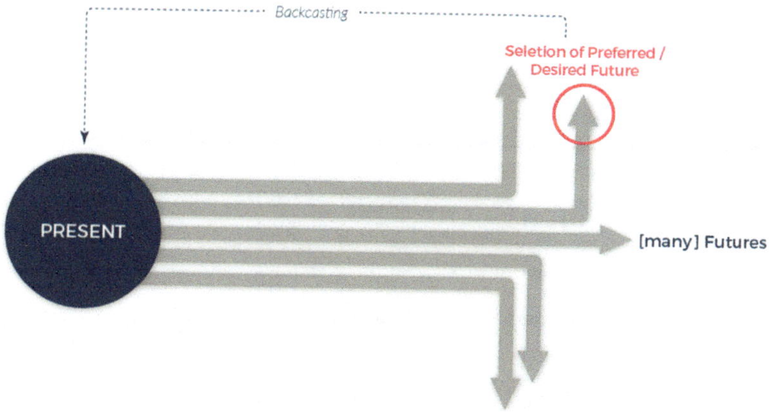

Fig. 3.2 Preferred future—selection from plausible alternatives; "…what does this (our preferred future) mean for our choice-making today?

with accumulated knowledge from several years of working experience on a related domain.

To set the appropriate expectations, it is important to highlight to the intended readership that this project initiative is not about prediction or crystal-ball gazing what the future will be. Instead, the overarching objective was to encourage participants and stakeholders to take an important first step toward *thinking about the future—continuously*. In other words, this study has been conceived on the premise that future outcomes can be influenced by the choices made in the present.

Therefore, we are mindful that choices made today (actions) will have consequences in the future, and, for these choices to be made responsibly and wisely, we need to select among many alternative futures (plural) and determine which future (singular) is desired (Fig. 3.2). Realizing this opportunity—that we can only influence what is "yet to be", while having to live with "what has already been", the determination of this project is to spark a mindset of action-oriented foresight that are manifested in business practices, which seek to move '…merely possible futures into the realm of plausibility, while generating knowledge that will bring them about as reality' [14].

3.2 The Delphi Panel Participants, and Survey Approach

As introduced earlier (Chap. 1), a total of 12 experts (10 from the Private Banking industry, and 2 from academia) took part in the initial scoping round of the survey. Extensive background research produced carefully constructed probing questions, to which the Delphi panel would be encouraged to respond creatively about current issues, and signals that point toward futures scenarios in 2020, and 2030. The results

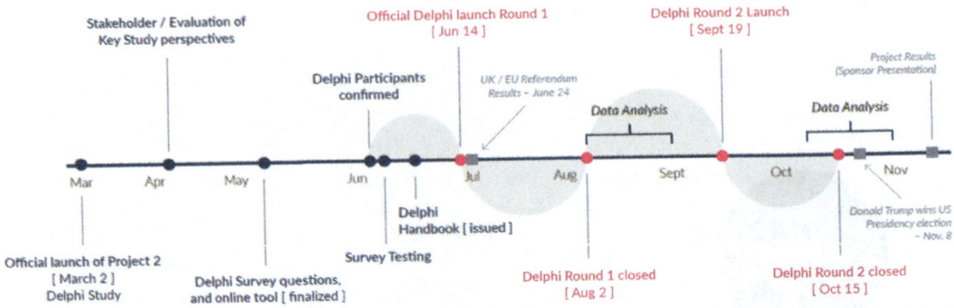

Fig. 3.3 Delphi survey—timeline and key milestones

of this process would form the combined knowledge, perspectives, and opinions from experts in private banking and social science, and the inputs obtained in the broader context of this study.

With the focus firmly placed on the future, qualitative research methods were considered as most appropriate, and to this end, the Delphi method was deployed as a proven forecasting technique to evaluate, and if required, to adapt the preparatory stages in conducting a design-inspired foresight study. Following this process, the anticipation was to gain invaluable insights into the experts' opinions, while eliciting the experts' understanding and rational applied to the situation being studied. The study design allowed each participant to share their views—openly and anonymously, about current issues that are determinants for continuous growth, and those practices that are seen as fading and thus should be considered for elimination. Looking further into the future, the inquiry was directed toward the year 2020 and 2030, asking Delphi participants to consider futures from four perspectives—the organization, market, industry, and the Chinese consumer.

While the overall project took nine months (March to November) to be completed (Fig. 3.3), the Delphi survey officially commenced on June 14th and ended on October 15th. Consensus toward important issues and the likelihood of their occurrences, was reached among the group of experts (7 from industry and 3 from academia) who participated in the second and final Delphi round.

3.3 The Delphi Survey Questions

Opening the Delphi survey (Round 1), the expert panel was asked to respond to the following questions:

(1) What are the important topics/issues that define the core of private banking that will need defending and keep extending?

(2) Which topics/issues do you see as fading and should be eliminated?

(3) When considering each of these four perspectives, what are the early signs that will potentially change the way and future **(2020 and 2030)** of private banking?

(a) the organization,
(b) the market,
(c) the industry,
(d) the Chinese consumer.

For questions 1 and 2, a minimum of 2 responses were sought; in response to questions 3 and 3.1 experts were then asked to nominate at least one issue and the rational for each of the four perspectives to the year 2020, and 2030. Thus, for each industry expert enrolled in the Delphi, a minimum of sixteen nominated issues were anticipated to emerge; at careful analysis of the first Delphi survey round, a total of 237 issues had in fact been identified. These issues (Table 3.1) were then cross-referenced and synthesised into 25 issue sub-groups (8 of these were considered as dominant among the group), 8 primary issue groups that would belong to four primary issue clusters (macro, consumer-driven, technology-based, and industry-directed impacts).

Based on a rigorous process of data sorting and coding, important themes (28) emerged. These were then given definitions to guide the analysis of data collected in consecutive rounds, hence ensuring consistency across the entire data coding process.

3.4 Delphi Round 1—Growth and Collapse Scenario Statements

After the first-round analysis was completed, Delphi panel participants were presented with statements for each of the scoping questions, now synthetized from the opinions of the experts. For example, responses received on issues in private banking that will need defending and keep extending (*Q.1*), the analysis produced the following statement that is reflective of the industry experts' current business perspectives that are determents for continuous growth:

> Private Banking (PB) services are intended to identify, protect, and grow diversified valuables and values of clients. PB localization (greater China) provides continuous advantages and the ability on differentiating itself from other PBs through client-centric advisory capabilities. Amidst on-going regulatory complexity and the lack of clarity (e.g. segregation of banks and securities, varying regional / local policy, rule-sets, foreign ownership restrictions, license requirements), successful players in Private Banking must continue to defend, or look for opportunities, which protect the interests against new Financial Services entrants (e.g. FinTech) and other non-banking brands (e.g. Alibaba's Ant Financial, Tencent's WeBank).

Following the same rigorous process, issues nominated by experts which point toward practices that are fading and should therefore be eliminated (*collapse*), the Delphi produced the following scenario statement:

Table 3.1 Delphi round 1—Issues by cluster, groups, Sub-groups, and those most dominant (frequency)

Issue cluster [4]	Issue groups [8]	Issue sub-groups [25]	Dominant issue sub-groups [8]
Industry (106)	1. Financial Services Industry (democratization) 2. Private Banking (Operating Model, Products)	1. Partnerships 2. Adaptability of Local/Global banking models 3. Competition 4. Products and Services 5. Value Innovation 6. Next-generation of financial services 7. WM Operating Model 8. eWealth Management	Competition (11) WM Operating Model (23)
Consumer (53)	3. Psychographic Change 4. Social / behavioural Change	9. New generation of digital transformed consumers 10. Rising Affluence 11. Increasingly Sophisticated Consumers 12. Assurance (clients) 13. Client Engagement 14. Consumer Behaviour 15. Consumer Values 16. Inequality 17. New Workforce Types	Next generation of digital transformed consumers (6) Consumer values (9)
Macro (42)	5. Financial Services Market 6. Global (growth/instability) 7. Regulatory (State Control)	18. Economic Development 19. Globalization 20. Monetary Policy 21. Regulatory Environment 22. Regulatory/Governance	Economic Development (10) Globalization (7) Regulatory Environment (18)
Technology (36)	8. Technological (growth/instability)	23. Technological Innovations 24. Systems Integration 25. Digital Transformation	Technological Innovations (22)

The current Private Banking model needs to be reinvented, as some of its current practices are fading. Such as the inefficient physical client on-boarding (vs. digital), and the know-your-customer (KYC) processes that are too cumbersome and diminishing margins due to homogeneous 'high-touch' service delivery. In addition, ineffective client segmentation (by assets vs. needs), low-margin execution-only type services, a centralized advisory model (e.g. via CIO) and insufficient IT funding, all impact the prevailing Private Bank's growth and revenues ambitions.

When analysing the results relating to issues that determine opportunities for growth, and the risks associated with retaining practices that no longer serve the current business environment, experts categorically felt that these were closely linked to prevailing advisory models, product and service propositions, industry democratization, and client engagement practices, which are concerning the Industry as a whole. Moreover, the expert panel had strong opinions toward the evolution of consumer-related social and behaviorial trends, which underpin the opportunities and risks associated to the current private banking landscape in greater China.

3.5 Delphi Round 1—2020 (2nd Horizon) and 2030 (3rd Horizon) Scenario Statements

Aside from nominating growth and collapse related issues, the Delphi panel in round one of the surveys, was asked to identify the early signs (weak signals) or indicators of change in trends and systems that would potentially change the future of private banking. To this end, experts were asked to consider each of the four perspectives—the organization, the industry, the market, and the Chinese consumer. Experts expressed—often in great detail, their individual opinions on what were the early signs that inform trends or sustained developments potentially affecting the status quo.

The Organization Perspectives

When analyzing the results from an organizational perspective within the 2020 horizon, the most dominant themes arising from the expert opinions are associated to the broader category of issues affecting the traditional operating model of the Private Bank. At a much deeper level, sub-themes emerged that were defining wealth management strategies, and the issues relating to talent or Human Capital. In fact, these were among the most frequently cited areas that the Delphi panel proposed could have considerable impact in the near-term future.

Within the same time horizon (2020), the experts also shared their opinions on issues that were closely linked to the technological advancements; for example, driving the need for global functional capabilities, and accelerating digital integration with solution-specific technology partners. Strong views toward innovation directed at consumer value propositions, and specifically, the rising demands toward product and service differentiation, stood out in context of the future organization.

When comparing the 2020 key findings with those that emerged in the longer-term view of the panel, the most frequently cited issues affecting the future PB in 2030 were those that remain closely linked to the Operating Model category. In fact, the need to continuously develop the total wealth management strategy of the organization was seen as important as the issues relating to the demands placed on human capital and the talent pool as a whole. In this forward-looking scenario, the experts furthermore emphasized the need to innovate around the consumer value proposition, which they see as changing rapidly in view of globalization, rising affluence, social and behavioral changes in the years ahead.

From the analysis of the Delphi survey round one, the following synthesized statements were the experts combined opinions in how the future Private Bank organization may look in 2020:

> In 2020, the Private Bank (greater China) is operating within an agile organizational structure, delivering value to all stakeholders through tailored and personalized products and service differentiation. The Private Bank is culturally adapt with streamlined client on-boarding and off-boarding processes. It provides intelligent automated 'robo' client advisory and self-service capabilities, while achieving higher margins through advisory value innovations. With powers shifting increasingly toward the consumer, however, the rise of non-traditional players (e.g. Alibaba, Tencent), and 3rd-party PB/WM service providers, adds fierce competition. The Private Bank is increasingly being challenged by technological innovations such as IoT (Internet of Things), AI (artificial intelligence) and big data analysis capabilities.

And, in 2030:

> In 2030, the traditional Private Bank (PB) (organization) has ceased to exist, while the PB 2030 has transformed into a highly streamlined business in geographical proximity to key markets. This future organization is supported by global systems and specialist teams deploying the highest standard of advisory services. These services are curated across a network of strategic partnerships, and through open architecture platforms, they offer holistic, lifestyle-related, and client-centric value propositions. Efficient and decentralized product development capabilities provide competitive advantages enabling the PB 2030 (greater China) to withstand challenges by external forces (e.g. FinTech).

Based on these expert accounts, the first Delphi round presented a clear picture on significant challenges ahead in both the near-term (2020), and specifically those that might define the future organization as envisaged toward the long-term horizon (2030). In fact, collectively, the Delphi experts foreshadowed a complete transformation from the current private banking model to one that might determine the Private Bank in 2030.

The Industry Perspectives

Beyond the organization perspectives, the Delphi also produced industry-directed insights that could shape the private banking sector. From this perspective, and within the 2020 horizon, the panel most frequently addressed issues that relate to technological advancements, and those that will drive innovations and digital transformations. While these trends were already present in the current industry environment, the effects of such forces were directly seen to impact the next generation of financial services, and the wealth management operating model overall.

Comparing these findings—specifically relevant to the industry at large, the Delphi participants placed an even greater focus on the product and service propositions as determinants of a successful future private banking model in 2030. Aside from frequently referencing the next generation of financial services, many experts spoke of the importance placed on value innovation when considering futures of the 2030 private banking industry in greater China. Issues pertaining to the technological advancements remained a focal point in the expert's opinions as to what may impact the long-term futures of the industry. Here, they expressed the view that innovation and digital transformations will continue to be the disrupters of the industry.

From the analysis of the round one Delphi survey, the following statements reflect the overall synthesis of the experts' opinions in how the private banking industry may be affected in 2020:

> In 2020, the traditional Private Banking industry continues to be challenged by new entrants and brand leaders (e.g. Alibaba / MyBank; Tencent / WeBank). They offer next generation financial services through advanced technological network integration, delivering innovative product solutions via partner service providers - offering client interactions via open platforms. Traditional incumbents that continue with legacy systems will struggle to cope with evolving external challenges. In order to compete against these new players who adopt digital and platform-based business models, Private Banks had to shift from a product to a client-focused operating model. They have largely digitalized and automated PB functions, and offer robo-advisory services for less complex tasks.

And, in 2030:

> In 2030, the Private Banking industry in greater China is operating in a much more deregulated and democratized market environment with reduced authorities extended to bank licensees. This forces PBs to adapt business models alleviated of non-core systems / services (e.g. via outsourcing of data mining, automation, artificial intelligent assistance) to reduce the need for human interactions across non-critical touch-points. Continued investments in revenue-producing innovation drivers lead to higher profit margins and further evolvement of the client advisory model. The PB of 2030 follows new sources of revenues via bespoke UHNW advisory services, while digital customer experiences have greatly improved through the elimination of language barriers via systems translation (e.g. Baibo, BableFish). Additional revenue streams have been created through client segmentation based on 'needs', which allows for services to be intelligently switched between robo-advisory automation and bespoke human advisory services.

The Market Perspectives

As these scenario statements reveal, challenges and opportunities were being envisaged that go beyond the organization, thus affecting the industry at large. Dynamisms too would be felt across the greater China market, and more specifically, its expanding population of consumers. To this end, experts gave detailed insights from a market perspective, and across the two horizons, 2020 and 2030. Frequently recorded views were those relating to issues associated with the economic development of the China region, and the resulting impacts on the Financial Services sector. Regulatory (State Control) issues would play a key role in the near-term (2020), and an increasingly democratized FS industry, according to the experts, would become the triggers for increased competition through next generation product and service innovations.

From the analysis of the Delphi survey round one, the following statements reflect the overall synthesis of the experts' opinions in how the greater China market may be affected in 2020:

> In 2020, China has become the largest market of high-net-worth individuals (approx. 3.88 million); it is dominated by local institutions capitalizing on this market as the primary profit growth engine against an otherwise volatile economic market norm. While increased competition from traditional (PBs) and non-traditional (third-party e-commerce) players

are determinants for profit margins, there is still no clear industry leader offering holistic wealth management advisory services. Hence, innovative products, high margin value-added services, and clever 'need-based' wealth management solutions are needed.

And, in 2030:

In 2030, the Private Banking market in greater China is driven by global (standardized) financial deregulation, market-oriented reforms, and the internationalization of the RMB (Chinese Yuan) inching steps closer to becoming the global reserve currency. This presents new opportunities, such as empowering successful Chinese PBs to expand globally, offering best-in-class solution platforms and lifestyle-related services with omni-channel capabilities. Consequently, increased competition from other PBs, and data-rich e-commerce juggernauts (e.g. Alibaba, Amazon, Facebook, Google) extending financial services management value propositions, are no match for traditional PBs to compete and remain viable.

Summarizing the market perspectives, the Delphi revealed that it is likely that Chinese PBs will lead global expansions, that consumer loyalty is no longer assured unless new value is added to their lives, and that markets will continue to be liberalized through globalization and deregulation transformation.

The Chinese Consumer Perspectives

From a design led innovation stance, an important perspective is that of the Chinese consumer. Here, the Delphi was to reveal insights from the expert group as to what are the drivers that will determine future consumer banking needs, or indeed their desires that may inform wealth management related propositions. From the analysis of the round one data, the most frequently cited issues were determinants of social and behavioral consumer changes. In fact, the panel raised the importance on consumer value perceptions, while similarly stressing rising affluence and inequality as important opportunities and concerns.

Looking further ahead to the year 2030, the Delphi panel anticipated changes in behavior that would define the next generation of financial services. Closely linked to this perspective were the panel's views on the future workforce and how this would become one of the biggest challenges the organization, and indeed the industry faces.

From this Delphi survey round analysis, the following statements reflect the overall synthesis of the experts' opinions in how the Chinese consumer may have evolved in 2020:

In 2020, the affluent Chinese consumer (Tier 1–3 cities) is better educated, lives in urban surroundings, has greater mobility and enjoys higher per-household discretionary spending. He aspires to improve himself and others (family), collectively they are influenced by peer-based recommendations, while in search for convenience and lifestyle (e.g. concierge, special events) integrated services.

And, in 2030:

In 2030, the affluent Chinese consumer is independent, better informed, highly mobile, digitally adept, and fully integrated into global society. This enables individuals and their families to live through mobile lifestyle choices, moving family and investments autonomously. With rising inequality remaining a widespread concern, affluent Chinese consumers are more selective about where they spend their money (domestic/international), on what (products/services/), and how (online/offline) they consume. They demand quality (products/services), convenience, and have a preference toward trusted brands that are transparent and genuine in their ethics and corporate social responsibility.

In Chap. 4 of this report the complete 2020 and 2030 scenario statements, and the Delphi panels' ratings of the likelihood of their occurrences, can be viewed.

This high-level summary are the findings synthesized from the expert responses to the Delphi survey Round 1. Based on these initial insights, a second Delphi survey round (2) was initiated. The focused of this Delphi round was to obtain the panel's feedback to each of the synthetized statements produced from the first round. The advantage of applying a Delphi technique lies in its ability to offer participating experts' sequential feedback during subsequent rounds of questioning. Not only can Delphi panel experts comment on each scenario statement, but they also have the opportunity to rate specific features contained within each statement perspectives for their likelihood of occurrence.

3.6 Delphi Round 2—Consensus Toward Futures Scenario Statements

At the outset of this second survey round, consensus among the Delphi panel was sought as to what are the desired futures that define private banking to the year 2020, and more importantly, the imaginary Private Bank proposition to the year 2030. Additional scenarios—relating to the same four perspectives of the organization, industry, market, and the Chinese consumer, were included in the survey as this would generate further insights from the opinions of the experts. While the panel's focus was primarily directed toward the 2030 futures, experts were given the opportunity to comment on each of the 2020 horizon statements. Additionally, they were asked to rate each of the 2020 statements for their likelihood of occurrence. The likelihood scale was introduced with clarity as to what the rating options and their specific meaning; "desirable, probable, plausible, possible" (see Fig. 3.3).

With the emphasis placed on the futures scenario statements to the year 2030, the panel was firstly asked to comment on the overall statements, and then rate the likelihood of occurrence of several specific features contained within the statement. This was to ensure a more in-depth response from the panel, subsequently confirming whether consensus was reached on the scenario statement features, and their likelihood of the occurrence. Additional scenarios were presented under each of the four perspectives, which the Delphi panel was asked to again rate, and provide further comments on.

From the analysis of the second and final Delphi round, the expert panel reached consensus on which of the scenarios were seen as shaping the futures of the Private Bank 2030 in greater China. After obtaining further comments to each of the statements presented in Round 2 of the Delphi, expert opinions relevant to the 2020-

and 2030-time horizons, are presented in form of modified statements, and their likelihood of occurrence, in Chap. 4 of this report.

Here, we summarize the four perspectives, and the likelihood of each statement feature presented to the expert panel for rating purposes. From an organizational perspective, for example, the Delphi revealed that the Private Bank in 2030 is highly streamlined, agile and dependent on physical advisory services located in key markets that cater to market-oriented consumer needs. In fact, a majority consensus (80%) was reached that the PB 2030 is likely to offer its customers lifestyle-oriented value propositions via user-centric, behavioral-driven touchpoints. Whether disruptive 'unicorn' start-up organizations will deploy gamification to entertain and educate their clients on financial management issues, or whether their systems are capable of colloquialisms (informal speech) and personal idiosyncrasies (personal traits) recognition optimization, was considered as equally desirable/probable and plausible/possible among the panel of experts.

The greater China market environment in which the future PB 2030 operates within, may to a higher degree of probability (60% of the expert participants rated this as desirable/probable) be subjected to global regulatory standardization, while an equally large percentage of the group were either undecided (20%) or considered it possible (50% responded that it might happen) that the RMB currency would have been fully internationalized, inching steps closer to becoming the global reserve currency in 2030. The expert panel also conceded that the market environment surrounding the PB sector will have experienced increased competition to an extend that smaller PBs will cease to exist. In fact, 60% of the Delphi panel considered smaller PBs to reach a point in the future where they are unable to compete with data-rich e-commerce (non-traditional FS providers) such as Alibaba, Amazon, Facebook, or Google).

From an Industry perspective, the analysis of opinions received from the experts as to whether the PB sector (or Financial Industry as a whole) is operating in a much more deregulated and democratized environment in 2030, half of the expert panel considered this scenario as plausible/possible. Conversely, 70% of the expert group envisaged as highly possible that the financial industry will experience non-core systems and commoditization of services most likely to be offered virtually. Similarly, 60% of the Delphi panel rated as desirable/probable new revenue streams that will have been created in 2030. These would be based on client segmentation by needs, and services that are intelligently switched between robo-advisory automation and bespoke humanized advisory service propositions.

In 2030, the Chinese consumer is most probably living through mobile lifestyle choices, moving family and investments autonomously. Among the findings derived from the panel's consumer perspectives, are evolving behavioral consumption patterns that will see consumer preferences to shift toward lifestyle-inspired services and experiences, surpassing the interests of accumulating material products and goods. Moreover, seventy percent of the panel consented that it is both desirable and probable for the Chinese consumer in 2030 to favor PBs that develop trust through their values as a corporate citizen, and the community support that impacts the overall brand reputation.

The extended study findings—presented in form of scenario statements, their likelihood of occurrence, and the Delphi panel experts' consensus toward the statement features and additional scenarios to the year 2030, are listed in Chap. 5 of this report.

Reference

Voros J (2003) A generic foresight process framework. Foresight 5(3):10–21

Chapter 4
Delphi Analysis—Desired Futures 2020, and 2030

Abstract In the chapter, a comprehensive view toward desired futures is presented in form of synthetized statements from four different perspectives (the organization, market, industry, and the Chinese consumer), which a group of experts considered as desired scenarios of the future Private Bank (PB) in 2020, and 2030. Consensus among the Delphi panel toward specific statement features are visualized (data visualization) by their mean scores, and the likelihood of their occurrences.

Keywords Delphi analysis · Design-inspired foresight · Scenario statements, · Data visualization

The experts' opinions toward desired futures of the Private Bank and Wealth Management 2020, and 2030 are presented in form of desired scenarios, and the likelihood of their occurrences.

Key findings from the Delphi survey were first introduced in the executive summary. In this section of the report, a comprehensive view toward desired futures is presented in form of synthetized statements from four different perspectives, which the group of experts considered as desired scenarios of the future PB in 2020, and 2030. Consensus among the Delphi panel toward specific statement features are shown in from of mean values, and the likelihood of their occurrences.

Likelihood Indicator

The overall mean score value is the total mean for each feature response, divided by the total count of responses received.

Consensus Indicator

Consensus is visualized based on the majority count between "desirable/probable", "plausible/possible", and "undecided".

J. H. Bühring, *Private Banking and Wealth Management Futures 2030*, SpringerBriefs in Finance, https://doi.org/10.1007/978-981-16-3395-9_4

The Organization in 2020

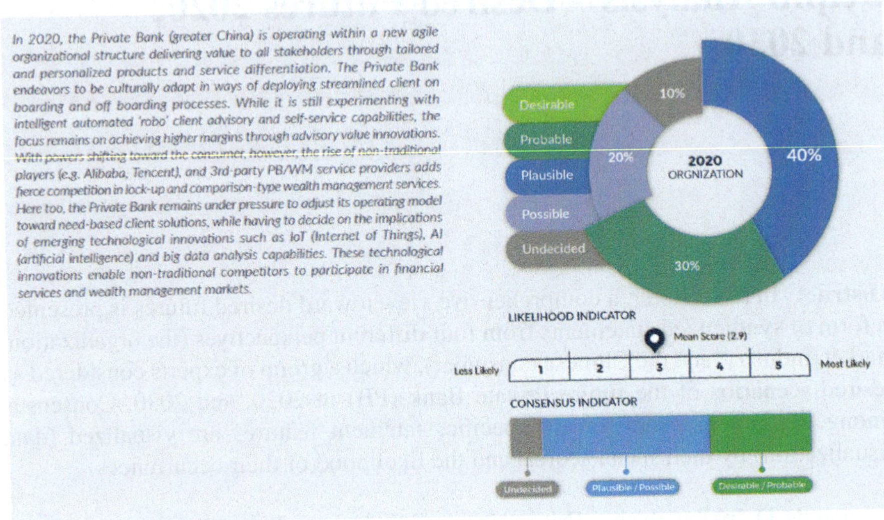

The Market in 2020

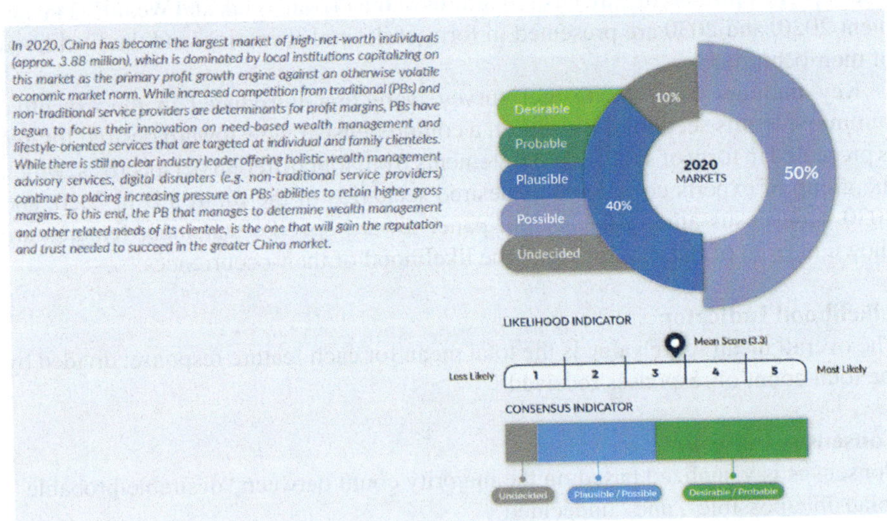

The Industry in 2020

In 2020, the traditional private banking industry continues to be challenged by on-going regulatory controls that could affect its profitability and hence overall attractiveness. Consequently, PBs are increasingly dependent upon the industry's ability to innovate in delivering bespoke WM, and HNW directed services that are focused on their clients' needs and personalization interests. Meanwhile, clients have become accustom to search and compare WM propositions based on perceived value and shared peer experiences; these growing consumer expectations have motivate new entrants and brand leaders (e.g. Alibaba / MyBank; Tencent / WeBank) to expand their service propositions to include financial services type solutions. As traditional incumbents continue the process of transforming their legacy systems, new industry entrants benefit from advanced technological development and network-integrating products that are considered (broadly speaking) as next-generation financial services. Those Private Banks successfully competing against these forces, have develop product differentiation based on human-level engagement, specifically around more complex wealth management solutions.

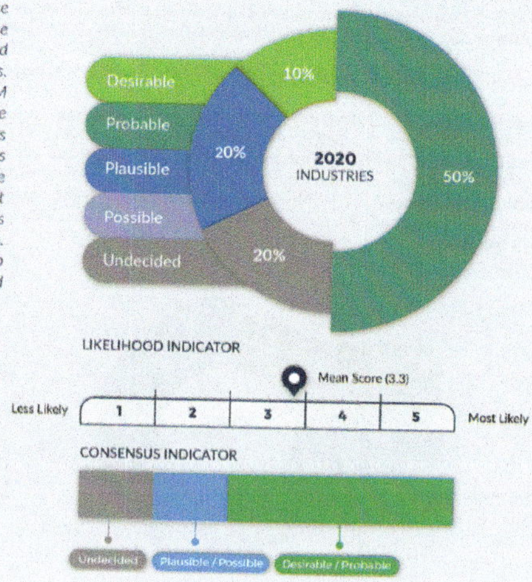

The Chinese Consumer in 2020

In 2020, the affluent Chinese consumer (affluence requires further definition, e.g. in context, and comparatively to more developed affluent markets) is better educated, lives in urban surroundings, and aspires greater regional and international mobility. Equally significant, however, is the mainstream consumer population defined by annual disposable incomes of RMB37,000 – 106,000; this consumer group will enjoy higher per-household discretionary spending power, which are the demand drivers for lifestyle related value-added services. These consumer populations may mature at a slower than expected rate; nonetheless, they aspire to improve themselves and the families that surround them.

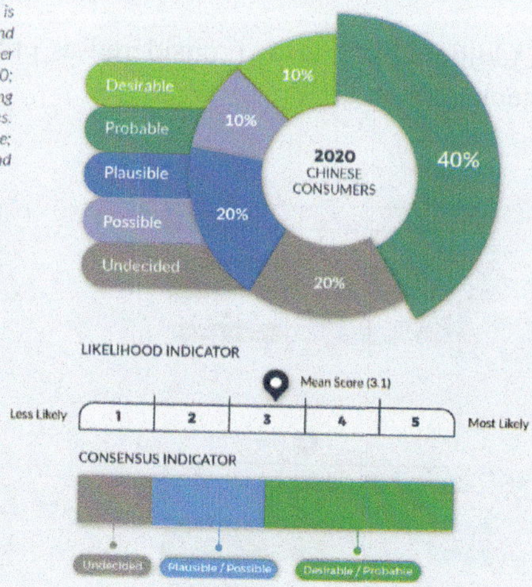

The Organization in 2030

In 2030, the traditional Private Bank (organization) has ceased to exist, while the PB 2030 operates through client-facing identities that are backed by powerful backend platforms, thus fully embracing the benefits of a highly streamlined entity with geographical proximity to key markets. This future entity is supported by global systems and specialist teams deploying the highest standard of wealth management advisory services. Operating within prevailing regulatory constraints, services are curated effectively across a network of strategic partnerships. Through open architecture platforms, the PB 2030 specializes in offering primarily investment management and advisory services, while some innovative players are experimenting with holistic, lifestyle-related, and behavioral-driven client touch-points most relevant to client interests and talents. To this end, efficient and decentralized product innovation capabilities will provide unique competitive advantages, which will enable the PB 2030 (greater China) to withstand challenges presented by external forces.

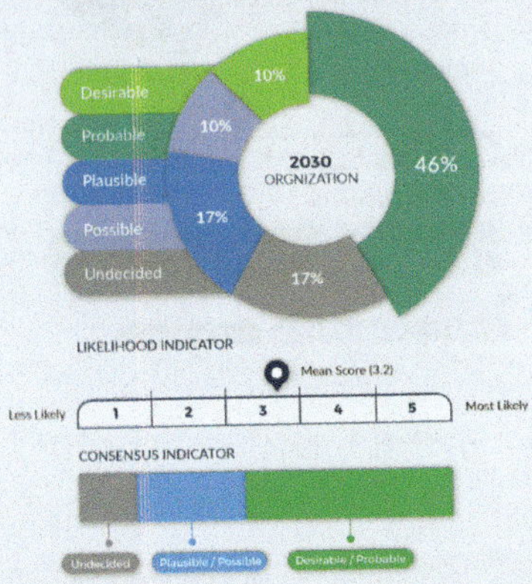

Feature 1: The PB is highly streamlined, agile and positions physical client advisory services in key markets to cater to market-oriented consumer needs.

Feature 2: Offers (via technology and content partnerships) lifestyle-related value propositions via user-centric, behavioral-driven touch-points.

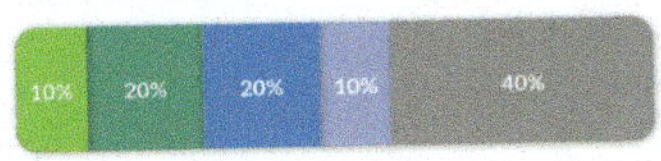

Feature 3: Disruptive 'unicorn' start-ups deploy e.g. gamification psychology to entertain and educate their clients on financial management issues, while their digital systems are capable of colloquialisms (informal speech), and personal idiosyncrasies (personal traits) recognition optimization.

Additional scenarios (considered as probable/desirable) that will define the PB Organization in 2030:

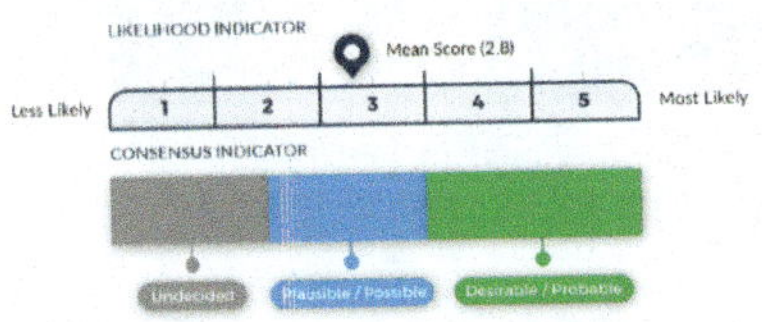

Added Scenario 1: Independent PB Advisors tap into open-platform hosts to offer their client tailored services and unique products.

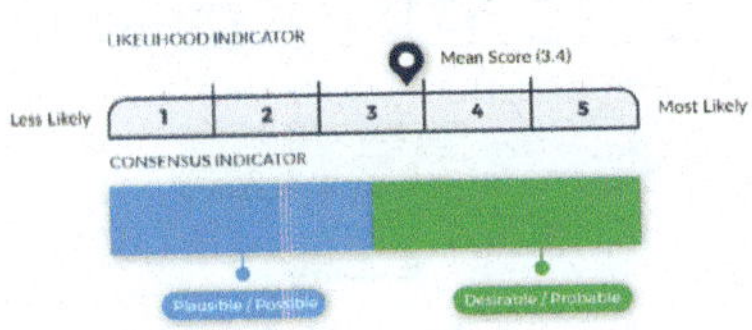

Added Scenario 2: Beyond its unique selling points and value propositions, the PB 2030 depends on a deep-seated brand identity to attract the attention of the Chinese consumer.

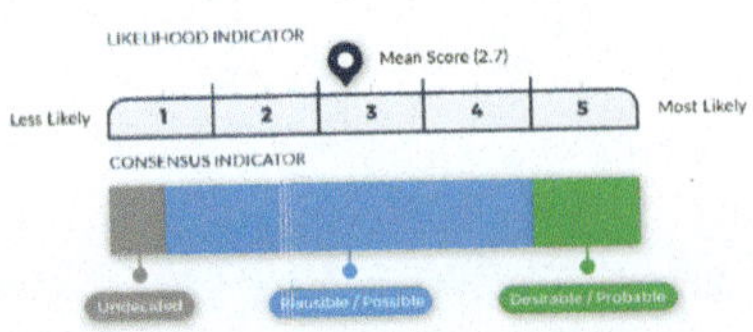

Added Scenario 3: The PB 2030 will depend entirely on its data analytics capabilities to create predictive and highly profitable products that are desirable across diverse client psychographics.

The Market in 2030

In 2030, the private banking market in greater China is increasingly driven by global (standardized) financial deregulation, market-oriented reforms, and the anticipated internationalization of the RMB (Chinese Yuan) as the global reserve currency. Chinese PBs may take this opportunity to expand their reach globally, offering consumers best-in-class solution and lifestyle-related services. Consequently, increased competition from other PBs, and data-rich e-commerce juggernauts (e.g. Alibaba, Amazon, Facebook, Google) who are in business to offer automated financial services and search-related value propositions.

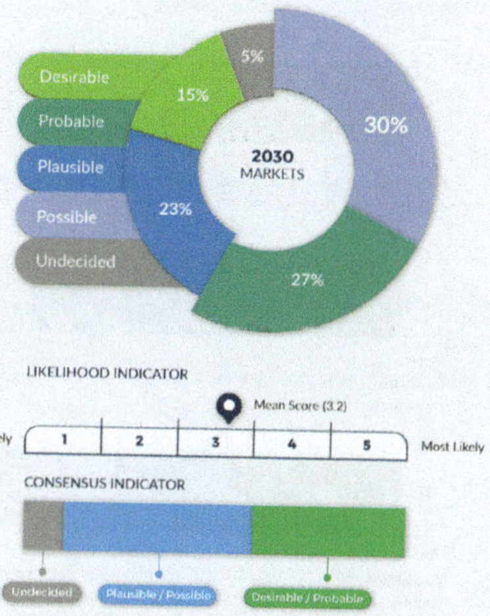

Feature 1: Global regulatory standardization (market liberalization).

Feature 2: The internationalization of the RMB currency.

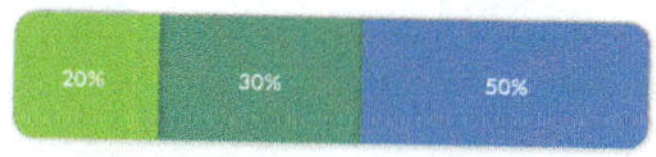

Feature 3: Chinese PBs are expanding globally.

Feature 4: Smaller PBs cease to exist, unable to compete with data-rich e-commerce (non-traditional Financial Services) players.

Additional scenarios (considered as probable/desirable) that will define the PB Organization in 2030:

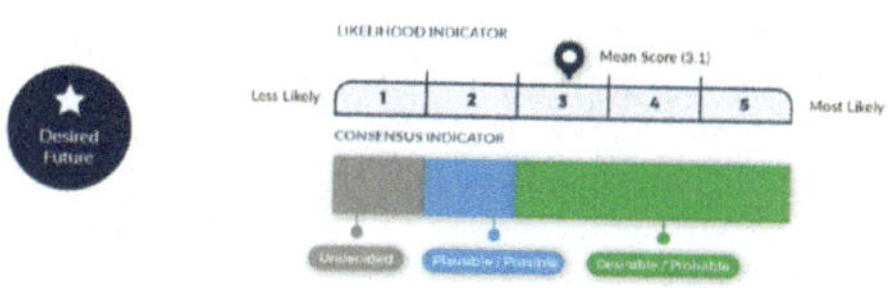

Added Scenario 2: Despite the aggressive entry of non-traditional players (e.g. Alibaba, Amazon, Google) aiming to capture a share of the wealth management market, the PB of 2030 differentiates itself from digital product solution providers, by offering physical face-to-face direct client advisory services designed to assist with complex investment decisions.

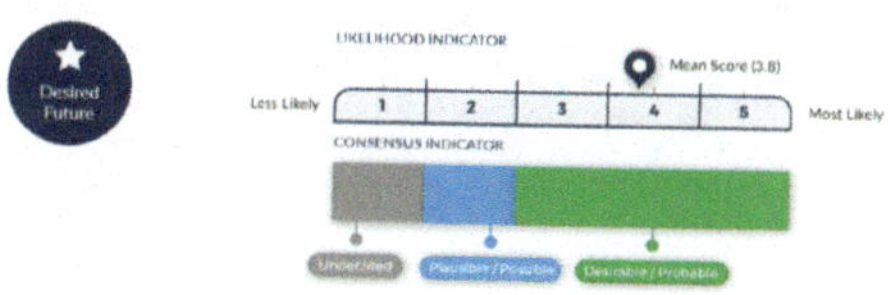

Added Scenario 4: Virtual PBs are established, providing technologically savvy Chinese consumers with fully integrated (e.g. SmartTablets, SmartTV, SmartWatch, VRDevice) digital/virtual customer-assistance experiences.

The Industry in 2030

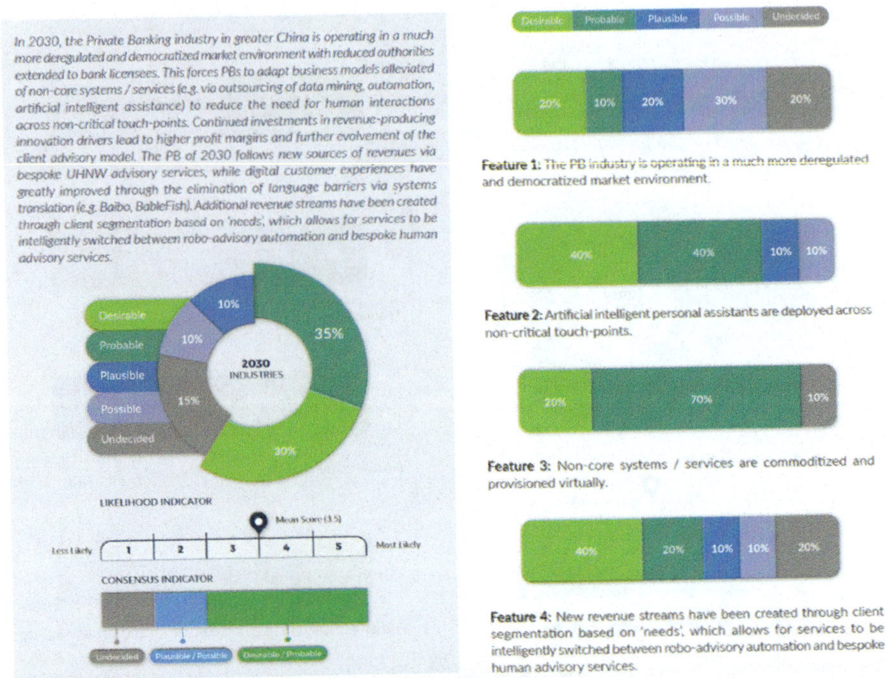

Additional scenarios (considered as probable/desirable) that will define the PB Industry in 2030:

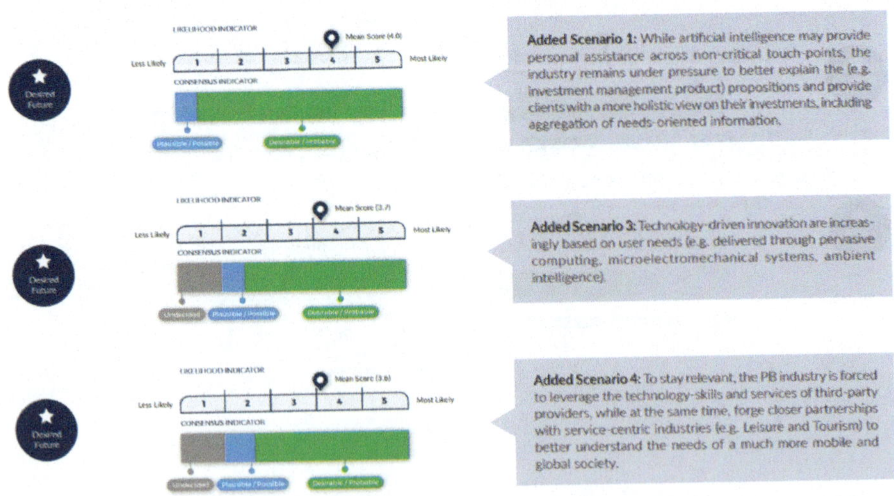

The Chinese Consumer in 2030

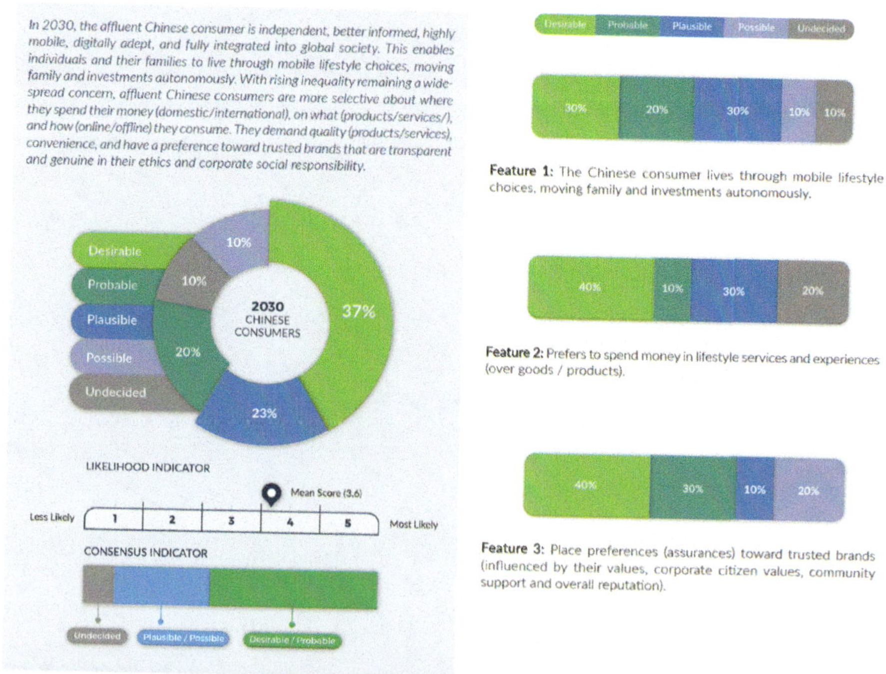

Additional scenarios (considered as probable/desirable) that will define the PB Consumer in 2030:

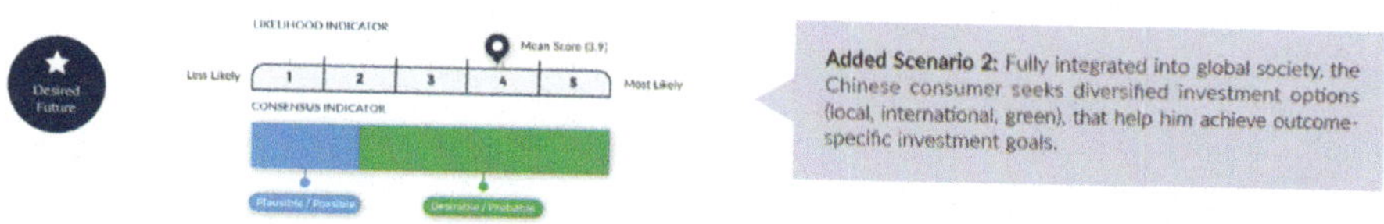

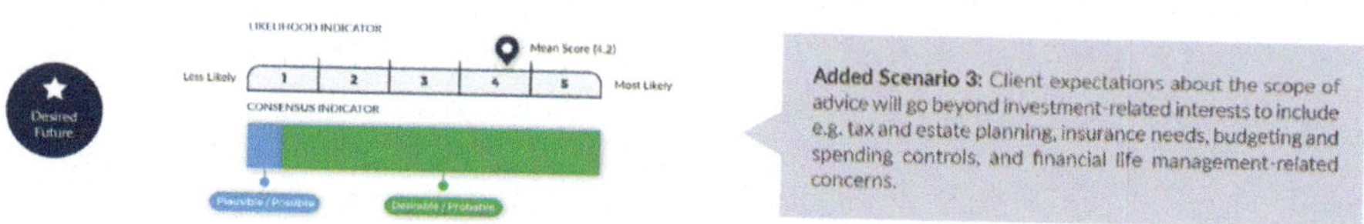

Chapter 5
Discussion and Implications

Abstract The results of the implementation of the Delphi method are discussed in this chapter; the methodology has proven its usefulness in this design-inspired foresight study involving experts who shared their opinions across a multitude of current and future perspectives. This novel approach has produced over 237 issues, which were grouped into four major issue clusters, comprising of eight distinctive groups, and 25 sub-issue groups. The study has demonstrated a general agreement among the experts that the current model of the private banking organization will cease to exist. Thus, foresight should be an essential part of organizational strategy, innovation, learning, navigating disruption, making sense of complexity, and adjusting to uncertain futures. The chapter concludes with implications, reported evidence in support of developing futures scenarios, and the primary considerations which this Design Foresight Delphi study addressed, are summarized.

Keywords Expert opinions · Visions · Strategic decisions · Uncertainty · Alternative futures · Implications · Futures considerations

A key objective of the Delphi study was to elicit specific insights derived from the opinions of a group of industry and academic experts, and their consensus as to the desired futures of private banking in greater China to the year 2030. As a result of the implementation of the Delphi technique, it was anticipated that important issues would emerge, and that themes derived from the experts' rationales would allow for insightful futures scenarios to be produced. From these scenario statements (current, 2020, 2030), collaborative learning was a key outcome, and, subsequently, it was the visions of these desired futures that would inform strategic and focused initiatives and their missions for design led innovations.

The literature reviewed during the course of this project confirmed the urgencies that business organizations, regardless of industry or size, are faced with. Indeed, concerns over unprecedented uncertainties in form of social analyses, globalization, and technology revolutions were frequently expressed by the expert participants in this study. The results presented in this report suggest that private banking stakeholders must rethink their business and operating models, the value propositions, and the organization's ability to invent toward desirable futures.

J. H. Bühring, *Private Banking and Wealth Management Futures 2030*, SpringerBriefs in Finance, https://doi.org/10.1007/978-981-16-3395-9_5

To this end, the Delphi methodology has proven its usefulness in identifying over 237 issues, which were grouped into four major issue clusters, comprising of eight distinctive groups, and 25 sub-issue groups. From the analysis of the expert rational for each of their nominated responses, 6 distinct theme categories, and their 28 sub-themes emerged. In total, 11 logical and useful statements were produced, which represent the desired futures scenarios based on the likelihood of continues growth and collapse, the near-term horizon of 2020, and the longer-term horizon to the year 2030.

The overall ratings of these futures scenarios, which were presented by each of their four perspectives, and the specific statement features contained within, show that all final scenario statements have been rated in the upper mean scores in relation to the likelihood of occurrence. This consensus-reaching outcome was anticipated considering the two-round process used and the nature of the Delphi method.

The study has demonstrated a general agreement among the experts that the current model of the private banking organization will cease to exist. In its place, the study findings foreshadow an overwhelming desire for the future Private Bank of 2030 to be highly streamlined, agile, while offering physical client advisory services in key market locations capable of responding to market-oriented consumer needs. Indeed, according to the experts, the future private banking organization will succeed if it can develop lifestyle related value propositions that respond to behavioural-driven and user-centric touch points, even if many of these service innovations will have to be sourced from third-party providers.

The Private Bank in 2030, furthermore, will likely have to compete for talent on regional and international levels. Experts seemed mindful that these are critical issues that must be addressed in ways which are impossible to imagine today, such as working with independent client advisors who offer their clients tailored services curated via open-platform hosts. Besides these human capital considerations, the future organization may face challenges and opportunities in its data analytics capabilities, which would be determinants for delivering desirable and profitable product innovations. Whether these data-driven competencies will be more advanced by non-traditional players and disruptive 'unicorn' start-ups, would be much less clear among the experts in this study.

The study has provided valuable insights into the market dynamics of possible futures affecting the PB to the year 2030. These, according to the experts, are least predictable when considering financial regulatory policies, global regulatory standardizations, or the impact of the RMB as the global reserve currency. Despite these uncertainties, however, the experts expressed strong desires to protect their interests in local and regional markets, by placing a greater focus on humanized client advisory service innovations that will set them apart from non-traditional players unable to assist their customers with complex investment decisions.

From an industry stand-point, the Delphi study gave solid insights into the evolving technological challenges that industry players are, and will continue to be faced with. Issues that can be seen as threats and opportunities were those closely linked to the advances in artificial intelligence. These technological developments could indeed play significant considerations in innovating tailored and need-based client experiences. Experts also agreed that a more holistic view on the clients' investments is needed. In fact, experts viewed this development as important considerations when delivering services, balancing between automation and humanization of future service propositions. These insights should be seen as early signs of significant shifts in technology-enabled service propositions, which not only address the increasing investment and lifestyle-oriented client needs, but similarly, the necessities of future PBs to generate new revenues through smarter, intelligent, and flexible applications.

It is widely anticipated that China will become a high-income country sometime before 2030, and the experts in this study expect the affluent Chinese consumer in 2030 as independent, better informed, highly mobile, digitally adept, and fully integrated into global society. The social science literature projects demographical shifts in form of gender, age, and overall diversity when comparing today's customer to the investor of 2030. However, a balanced view on client and prospect populations is recommended, as the needs of younger generations (e.g. Millennials) may differ greatly to those of an aging population such as the baby boomer generation increasingly becoming depend on longer-term savings and investment propositions. In context of the Chinese consumer markets, it is here that the Delphi revealed consensus among the experts who see clients seeking diversified investment options that address outcome-specific goals, including tax and estate planning, insurance, budgeting and spending controls, and financial life management service offerings.

Implications

Foresight should be an essential part of organizational strategy, innovation, learning, navigating disruption, making sense of complexity, and adjusting to uncertain futures. Significant drives of change are underpinning this Ignite Innovation Industry-University partnership program, as we recognize the value of exchanging insights, foresight, strategy, and innovation knowledge.

As design and innovation are becoming increasingly synonymous in both meaning (e.g., Design Thinking) and reach (e.g., products, services, business models, ecosystems, etc.), the priority task of the world's top management, economic, and educational leaders is to effectively manage knowledge and to generate an innovative (corporate/community/learning) culture.

Similarly, new business perspectives are needed to prepare for alternative futures (e.g. define, design, prototype, and testing), as these futures will bring about substantial shifts in the mind of the advanced and very well informed consumer. Indeed, a consumer who will seek an active role in the decisions critical to themselves, their children, family, future generations and the environment that surrounds them.

There is a perceived failure in traditional approaches to strategic planning activities, as evidenced by numerous examples in recent history, and of firms who are no longer able to compete in an uncertain and increasingly globalized world. As this study set out to accomplish, was to position the value of design-inspired foresight as informants for design led innovation, thus improving an organization's learning to adopt new methods in their innovation practices.

In conclusion, the significance of this project initiative, and the research into desirable futures of private banking in greater China 2030, is fully recognized. Beyond the research findings reported here, this study was envisaged to continue this program by engaging with relevant stakeholders, and to transform the research findings into design led innovation opportunities. Combining the insights gained, a passion for meaning, the inter-relationships between issues and themes, and the future scenarios presented herein, the outcome of this Delphi research ought to address the following four primary considerations:

- How the future Private Bank (2030) will need to revolutionize the client experience in the face of rapid technological advancements that are threatening the relevance of the traditional banking delivery channels.
- How the entry of new and existing non-traditional banking providers is challenging the traditional banking system, and how Private Banking (2030) will need to respond to this challenge.
- How Private Banking (2030) will need to balance "people" and "systems" to engage and interact with next generations of HNW clients.
- How Private Banking (2030) will have evolved as a trusted financial partner, offering high levels of customization, and incentives to be measured based on performance and [value-generating] experiences.

Chapter 6
Methodology

Abstract In this final chapter, the design-inspired foresight approach is presented; this includes the preparations needed to engage with, and indeed, prepare, a panel of experts by adopting a design-inspired foresight process. Other success criterion are presented, and a step-by-step approach is discussed; this includes inspirations for critical thinking techniques, online survey tools, data analysis frameworks, and suggestions for post Delphi activities leading toward inventions of preferred, or indeed, desirable futures.

Keywords Delphi handbook · Participants preparations · Futures thinking · Creative thinking · Survey tools · Data analysis · Three horizons · Backcasting

To assist the Delphi expert panel in their thinking of future possibilities, and thus formulating their question responses in the survey, the project was guided by a number of proven foresight frameworks and methods that help identify, map, and create alternative futures—or indeed scenarios of desired futures.

6.1 The Delphi Handbook

It was deemed important to prepare each participant officially enrolled in this study, ahead of commencing with the Delphi. To this end, a "**Delphi Information Handbook**" was prepared and issued to each panel expert at least two weeks prior to the official first round launch. The objective was to present experts with a foundational futures question that was intended to start the conversation from a known perspective of the present, such as dealing with trends, issues, and the official version of the future. Additionally, some useful supporting materials were included; these had been curated primarily to open the panel's mind, and to start thinking about images of the future.

J. H. Bühring, *Private Banking and Wealth Management Futures 2030*,
SpringerBriefs in Finance, https://doi.org/10.1007/978-981-16-3395-9_6

Delphi Information Handbook

Delphi Information Handbook

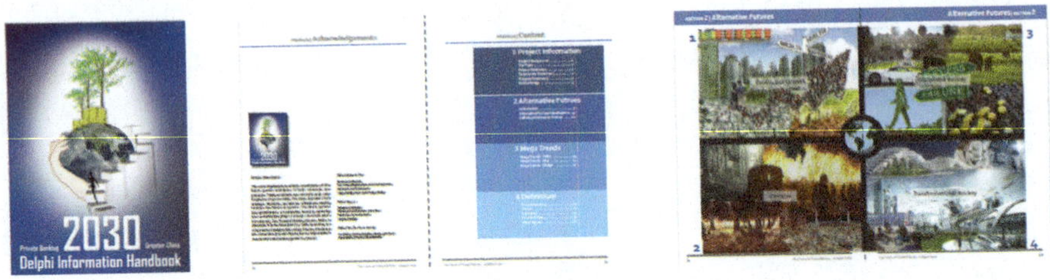

The [Foresight] Framework

Each question set was carefully prepared—balancing the project aims and objectives against the constraints of the experts' valuable time.

The purpose of deploying a foresight process is to move away from traditional means of predicting the future based on current knowledge. Instead, the focus is placed on creative imaginations of alternative futures. In other words, if we want to change our forecasts or imaginations about the future, then we need to understand how to change and transform our way of knowing the future from today's present way of knowings (Inayatullah 2008).

Alternative futures which can be considered aligned, are indeed more relevant or deeply more meaningful. Summarizing, here are some important insights into why we ought to do futures thinking and strategic foresight, and what can be some of the effects if we do:

- futures thinking challenges our dominant way of knowing and learning about the future
- futures thinking helps us see the world differently
- futures thinking is designed to help us rethink the present
- futures thinking is not intended to help us predict anything
- futures thinking helps us understand relationships between other ways of knowing the future AND why certain dominant or default perspectives about the past, present and future prevail
- futures thinking helps us understand the history of the future
- futures thinking challenges structures that inhibit or contain and seeks to evoke influence through agency
- futures thinking helps us aligned our personal narrative to strategy desired futures.

Creative Thinking

The work of de Brabandere and Iny (2013) challenges the conventional phrase of "thinking outside the box", in that we are merely moving from one existing mental image [box] to another, without creating a new box. In other words, without inventing new models, scenarios, or boxes, we will fail to imaging new possibilities. For example, instead of thinking "how to solve the problem of producing low-cost pens", ***Bic*** [the French stationary company] created a 'new box' by adopting a radical perspective. While ***Bic*** could have viewed itself as a pen company, it started to think of itself as a disposable-objects company that makes mass-produced inexpensive plastic implements (e.g. razors, lighters, etc.).

Brabandere poses a further challenge for us to think creatively. To illustrate the argument, think: "An example of a car is …"? It's easy to answer this question, because the number of answers is limited to the amount of car makers: Volkswagen, Ford, Toyota, and so on. The second question was not as straightforward: "A car is an example of …?" Here, the range of potential answers is unlimited: a car could be an example of mobility, status, or desire but also of danger, accidents, or pollution.

When you see a car as an example of mobility, not status, you could conclude that there might be people for whom the utility offered by a car eclipses the status conferred by its possession. With that lens, start-ups like ***Uber*** begin to make a lot of sense. You could also think of a car as an example of transportation and delivery. And suddenly you have ***Uber*** drivers delivering parcels and posing a threat to logistics companies.

So, ask yourself, *"A Private Bank is an example of …?"*.

6.2 The Delphi—Online Survey Tool

The Delphi was conducted in an online, web-based environment, using a professional research platform called *"Qualtrics"*. Each Delphi expert was issued access details to the survey site, allowing them to answer survey questions at their own convenience. It was anticipated that some experts may travel frequently; hence, an off-line survey questionnaire equivalent was made available to them. Additional support was offered throughout the survey stages, providing important guidance for each iteration in order to complete the survey rounds in a timely manner. The Delphi Handbook was designed to assist experts in their thinking of the future; some content was based on imagery—others relate to commonly reported Mega Trends.

6.3 The Delphi Analysis

To help us make sense of possible futures, this Delphi employed the Alternative Futures method developed by Jim Dator at the Hawaii Research Center of Futures Studies. Specifically, the study focused on two out of the four generic futures, namely *"growth"* and *"collapse"*.

Continuous Growth

A future that manifests the results of current trends and conditions, extrapolated forward. Continued growth is the "official" view of the future of all modern governments, educational systems, and organizations. The purpose of government, education, and all aspects of life in the present and recent past, is to build a vibrant economy, and to develop the people, institutions, and technologies to keep the economy growing and changing, forever. This includes both positive and negative growth.

Collapse
A future in which major social systems are strained beyond the breaking point, causing system collapse and social disarray. Collapse driven by resource shortages, food shortages, climate change, environmental disasters, widespread natural or human-made diseases, earthquakes, volcanic eruptions and other acts of god. Political or administrative ineptness or a snowballing series of pure accidents or terroristic events, nuclear war or some combination of these lead to a slide of our present high civilization into conditions not unlike the early Dark Ages in Europe—or worse.

Foresight Methods

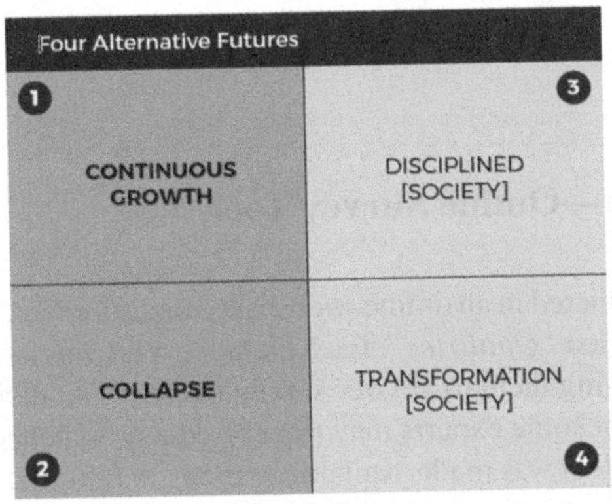

Question directed at the future (2020, and 2030) were analyzed based on the futures-oriented Three Horizon model (Fig. 6.1). The First Horizon represents the current prevailing system as it continues into the future, which loses fit over time as its

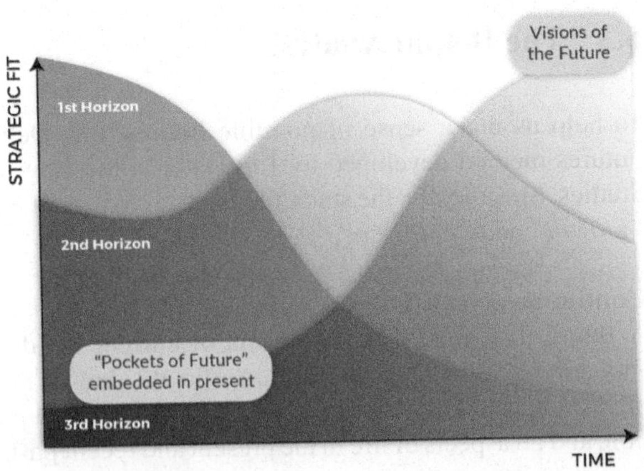

Fig. 6.1 Schematic of the futures-oriented Three Horizons model, 2008 adapted from Currey and Hodgson ()

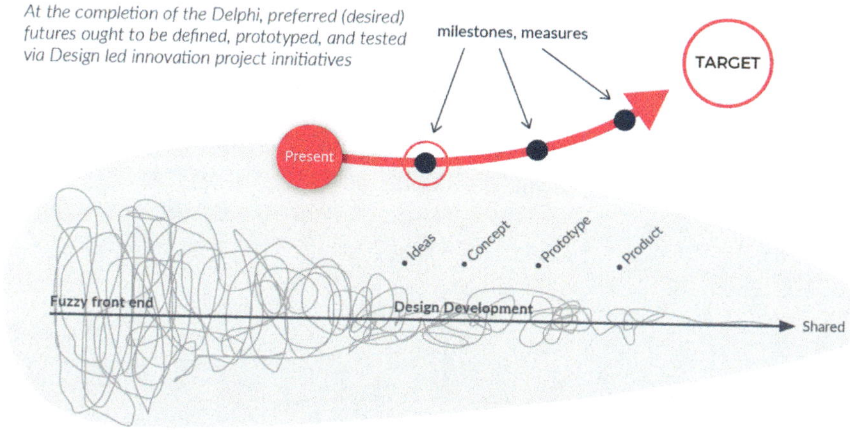

Fig. 6.2 Backcasting method applied to milestones toward a preferred future

external environment changes. The '3rd Horizon captures ideas or arguments about the future of the system which are, at best, marginal in the present, but which over time may have the potential to displace the world of the first horizon, because they represent a more effective response to the changes in the external environment. While the 2nd Horizon captures the intermediate space in which the first and third horizons collide. This is a space of transition which is typically unstable. t is characterized by clashes of values in which competing alternative paths to the future are proposed by actors.

Post Delphi Expectations

At the completion of the Delphi, and the careful analysis of the survey results that produced valuable insights toward alternative (and desirable) futures, it is anticipated that the findings will allow design led innovation projects to be defined through a "backcasting" technique. This process can lead toward inventing (visualizing and demonstrating) stages (or milestones) leading toward a preferred future scenario (Fig. 6.2).

References

De Brabandere L, Iny A (2013) Thinking in new boxes: a new paradigm for business creativity. Random House.

Curry A, Hodgson A (2008) Seeing in multiple horizons: connecting futures to strategy. J Fut Stud 13(1):1–20

Inayatullah S (2008) Six pillars: futures thinking for transforming. Foresight 10(1):4–21

The manufacturer's authorised representative in the EU is Springer Nature Customer Service Centre GmbH, Europaplatz 3, 69115 Heidelberg, Germany. If you have any concerns regarding our products, please contact ProductSafety@springernature.com

Printed and bound by CPI Group (UK) Ltd, Croydon, CR0 4YY
30/09/2026
02225261-0002